Between Scylla and Charybdis

The Army of Elector Friedrich August II
of Saxony, 1733–1763

Part I: Staff and Cavalry

Marco Pagan

Helion & Company

Helion & Company Limited
Unit 8 Amherst Business Centre
Budbrooke Road
Warwick
CV34 5WE
England
Tel. 01926 499 619
Fax 0121 711 4075
Email: info@helion.co.uk
Website: www.helion.co.uk
Twitter: @helionbooks
Visit our blog at http://blog.helion.co.uk/

Published by Helion & Company 2018
Designed and typeset by Mach 3 Solutions Ltd (www.mach3solutions.co.uk)
Cover designed by Paul Hewitt, Battlefield Design (www.battlefield-design.co.uk)
Printed by Henry Ling Limited, Dorchester, Dorset

Text © Marco Pagan 2018
Original colour artwork © Franco Saudelli 2018; black and white artwork as credited.
Maps by George Anderson © Helion & Co. 2018

Cover: 'The City of Dresden', hand-coloured engraving, © Anne S.K. Brown Collection

ISBN 978-1-912174-89-8

British Library Cataloguing-in-Publication Data.
A catalogue record for this book is available from the British Library.

For details of other military history titles published by Helion & Company Limited, contact the
above address, or visit our website: http://www.helion.co.uk

We always welcome receiving book proposals from prospective authors.

In loving memory of my parents Claudio Pagan (1930–1989)
and Loredana Giraldi Pagan (1932–2017)

Contents

Author's Preface

Since I was a child, I heard about Meissen porcelain, my mother being a professional painter and a teacher of porcelain painting. I will always remember her sitting hours and hours at her desk in the crouched position she was able to maintain, covering exquisite porcelain objects of different shapes with carefully studied composition of flowers or monochrome landscapes. While she was at work, defining herself just as an artisan, she was still able to answer all my questions, just asking for a moment of pause when the work required her full attention. She talked about everything, history, religion, art, travels. She had travelled a lot during her life. A curious boy, I was always eager to learn and I was really delighted by her lessons. I could hear her slow and gentle speaking for hours. I learned about Meissen, near Dresden, where the production of European porcelain started in 1710 and attracted artists and artisans to establish one of the most famous porcelain manufactures.

Growing up, I developed an instinctive relationship with distant Saxony. The Saxony of the eighteenth century was a real heaven for the European artists. The voyagers of the age bucolically described the country as a luxuriant garden punctuated by fabulous private residences. Since the middle of the century, the tour guides prescribed a visit of the capital, Dresden, and of the marvellous Royal Collections. The Saxon people loved their rich territory as much as they enjoyed the life and the arts. As part of the Holy Roman Empire, the Electorate of Saxony had an army, but the Saxon never cultivated military ambitions. Augustus 'the Strong' had travelled and visited the France of the Sun King and, flabbergasted by the richness of its culture, introduced the arts to the Electorate and promoted a general modernization. Saxony could not be more different from her Prussian neighbour. Saxony easily exchanged fully equipped soldiers for rare China pottery in Prussian hands. The Saxon army normally averaged 20,000 men and when needed this could at best be doubled; the poorer Prussia could field ten times this number. With such a neighbour, a crisis could be foreseen.

Saxony's ruling House of Wettin was universally criticized for siding with Prussia, France and Bavaria against Maria Theresa's army, but none could forget the heavy French influence on the matter. Soon the Elector and the Saxon court realized that the real problem was their aggressive ally. The Prussians were always harsh with the Saxons even before the change of the alliances. The Prussians considered the Saxon army as constantly weak, extending this criticism to the whole population. King Friedrich of Prussia in particular had a deep resentment toward Saxons and Saxony. We know some of the causes of this somehow irrational resentment but some are still unclear and matter of debate. There is scarce need to mention the Prussian army, the personified symbol of the militarism of the eighteenth century. The allied powers of France, Austria, and Russia managed to keep this perfectly drilled army at bay during the Seven Years War, defined as a 'first world war'; but Prussia, even if bloodied, survived.

The Saxon army reorganized by Augustus 'the Strong' and inherited by his weak and limited son served its country during the Polish Succession War, the First and Second Silesian Wars. The Prime Minister Count Heinrich Brühl, much more determined to hunt for artistic masterpieces for himself and his master than to defend his motherland, reduced the army to an ineffectual minimum strength and in 1756, it was simply no match for the Prussians. The aim of this work, dedicated to all lovers of military matters, history, and wargames, is to accompany Franco Saudelli's military artwork. We never had the ambition to cover the topic in the most exhaustive way but we hope to be successful in just giving to the readers a chance to travel back in the past and partially explore an almost forgotten army.

Foreword by Richard Couture

This work on the history and organisation of the Saxon Army between 1733 and 1763 by Dr Marco Pagan fills an important gap in the documentation available in English on this topic. Prior to this publication, readers had to rely mostly on German sources. Furthermore, both volumes come with wonderful uniform plates from the very talented Franco Saudelli.

As coordinator of the wiki 'Kronoskaf – Project Seven Years War' for more than ten years, I have had the opportunity to work with a large number of collaborators and have constantly been astounded by their knowledge, dedication, and generosity. There are so many of them that I cannot even start to enumerate them here. However, I can certainly say that the team formed by Dr Marco Pagan and Franco Saudelli definitely belongs to this list of outstanding collaborators. Their numerous contributions have significantly improved several articles of our wiki. I seize the occasion that is given to me to thank them for their incredible enthusiasm and generosity.

Dr Marco Pagan and Franco Saudelli are not at their first publication. They both have a marked interest in military history. Dr Pagan, a long-time member of 'La Sabretache', a society for military history studies, has already published a dozen of articles on related subjects in the international edition of the Italian Magazine 'Soldatini'. His elegant and factual writing style makes for a very enjoyable and informative reading.

For his part, Franco Saudelli is a very well-known artist who collaborated with all the articles of Dr Pagan and who works mainly for Bonelli Edition, a well-known Italian comic publisher. He produced a dozen of 'Dylan Dog' volumes and recently, in the historical series, *La battaglia di Marengo* a wonderful masterpiece. At first glance, you will be able to appreciate Franco's quite unique style and will ask for more of his very peculiar uniform plates where each character has his own strong personality.

Richard Couture – Coordinator of 'Kronoskaf – Project Seven Years War'
(www.kronoskaf.com/syw)
Montreal, Canada

Introduction

On 1 February 1733, King Augustus II 'The Strong' of Poland suddenly died, at Warsaw. As Friedrich August I, he was also Elector of Saxony. The Polish crown could not be simply inherited and the King was elected by an assembly of the country's noblest families. The legitimate son of the dead sovereign succeeded him in Saxony as Elector Friedrich August II, but could not automatically be the new King of Poland. Poland at this time, or the Lithuanian-Polish Commonwealth, was anything but a united country. Luckily for the new Elector, the 33-year-old Heinrich von Brühl was in Warsaw. This young nobleman had advanced rapidly in his political carrier. He was commissioned *Kammerjunker* in 1727 and with the benevolence of the Elector rapidly rose to the rank of *Kammerpraesidenten* only three weeks before the Elector's death. He acted rapidly and managed to secure the throne of Poland for his new master. On 23 June 1733, Brühl was *Kabinettsminister*.

August 'the Strong' left to his heir a well-equipped army of 30,000 men that could match the other European armies. This instrument of war was created in the period 1717–1730 by *Feldmarschall* von Flemming. When the War of Polish Succession sparked up, the army quickly mobilized. It was well prepared to defend the Elector's interests. Operating in conjunction with the Russian Imperial army and with the help of Austria, Friedrich August II of Saxony was crowned King Augustus III of Poland. His reign lasted until 1763.

The comparatively small Saxon army has received scarce or limited consideration in the past. To prepare an accompanying text for Franco Saudelli's artwork offered to me the opportunity to give a sight inside almost forgotten pages of history. This is a history of the Saxon army that fought, in a period of 30 years, four major wars.

Timeline

1733

1 February: Elector Friedrich August I of Saxony, King Augustus II of Poland, also known as 'August the Strong', dies at Warsaw. His legitimate heir is his son, the Elector Friedrich August II of Saxony.

16 July: Saxony fails to recognize the Pragmatic Sanction.

5 October: an extraordinary *Sejm* elects Friedrich August II of Saxony as King Augustus III of Poland.

10 October: start the War of Polish Succession.

1734

17 January the Elector Friedrich August is crowned as King Augustus III in Kraków.

1735

End of the War of Polish Succession.

1736

The official *Sejm* confirms the election of the King of Poland.

1740

31 May: King Friedrich Wilhelm of Prussia dies. His son succeeds him as Friedrich II.

20 October: Kaiser Karl VI passes away without a male heir. His daughter Maria Theresa (1717–1780) succeeds him. Bavaria, Saxony, France, Spain, and Prussia do not recognize her as Empress. Start of the War of Austrian Succession, also known as the Silesian Wars.

16 December: the Prussian army enters Silesia.

1741

16 February: Alliance of Dresden against Austria.

10 April: Battle of Mollwitz; Prussian victory over Austria.

9 October: Truce of Klein Schellendorf.

26 November: French and Saxon troops lay siege to Prague.

1742

25 January: Karl VII of Bavaria is elected Kaiser.

14 February: Austrian troops enter Bavaria and besiege München.

17 May: Battle of Chotusitz, Prussian victory over Austria.

28 July, Peace of Berlin; end of the first Silesian War. Silesia remains in Prussian hands.

1744.

Start of the Second Silesian War. Campaigning in Bohemia and retreat.

1745

20 January: Kaiser Karl VII dies.

4 June: Battle of Hohenfriedberg; Prussian victory over Austrians and Saxons.

13 September: Francis I (1708–1765), Maria Theresa's husband, is elected Kaiser.

30 September: Battle of Soor; Prussian victory over Austrians and Saxons.

October: the Saxon army is camped near Lipsia; Menzel, Brühl's chancellor, is discovered to be a Prussian spy.

15 December: Battle of Kesselsdorf; Prussian victory over Saxons.

25 December Peace of Dresden. Silesia is in Prussian hands. Friedrich II recognizes Francis I as German Kaiser.

1746

May: *Feldmarschall* Johann Adolf II of Sachesen-Weissenfels dies; *General-Lieutenant* von Rutowsky succeeds him as commander-in-chief.

1753

The Saxon army is severely reduced.

1754

1 January: the four *Generalate* of the Saxon army are reduced to two.

1756

2 July: Rutowsky realizes that the Prussian Army is on the move.

10 September: the Saxon army retires to Pirna.

1 October: Battle of Lobositz, Prussian victory over Austria.

16 October: the Saxon army surrender in Lilienstein.

20 October: Friedrich August II flees with Brühl and two sons to Warsaw.

1757

6 May: Battle of Prague, Prussian victory over Austria.

18 June: Battle of Kolin, Austrian victory over Prussia.

30 August: Battle of Gross-Jägersdorf, Russian victory over Prussia,

24 September: Menzel is sentenced to imprisonment for life.

5 November: Battle of Rossbach, Prussian victory over France.

22–25 November: Battle of Breslau, Austrian victory over Prussia.

5 December: Battle of Leuthen, Prussian victory over Austria.

1758

1 May: Prussian offensive in Moravia.

1 July: Siege of Olmütz.

25 August: Battle of Zorndorf, Prussian victory over Russia.

14 October: Battle of Hochkirch, Austrian victory over Prussia.

1759

23 June: Battle of Kay; Russian victory over Prussia.

12 August: Battle of Kunersdorf, Austro-Russian victory over Prussia.

20–21 November: Expedition of Maxen, Prussians under Finck surrender; Dresden besieged.

1760

14 June: Friedrich II besieges Dresden.

21 July: Severe damaging of the old town is caused by bombardments.

15 August: Battle of Liegnitz, Prussian victory over Austria.

9–13 October: Berlin under siege by Russians and Austrians.

3 November: Battle of Torgau, Prussian victory over Austria.

1761

20 August–26 September: Saxon army encampment near Bunzelwitz.

1762

5 January: Empress Elizabeth of Russia dies and is succeeded by Peter III.

5 May: Peace of Petersburg between Prussia and Russia.

19 June Alliance between Russia and Prussia; 20,000 Russian troops march against the Austria.

28 June: Catherine II succeeds Peter III after a coup.

21 July: Battle of Burkersdorf, Prussian victory over Austria.

29 October: Battle of Freiberg, Prussian victory over Austria.

25 November: ceasefire between Prussia and Austria.

31 December: preliminaries of peace start between Prussia, Austria, and Saxony.

1763

10 February: the Peace of Hubertusburg ends the Seven Years War.

30 April: Elector Friedrich August II returns to Saxony.

5 October: Death of Friedrich August II; his son succeeds him in Saxony as Elector Friedrich Christian.

28 October: Brühl dies in Dresden.

23 December: Death of Elector Friedrich Christian; his successor is only 13 years old and Prinz Xaver is proclaimed Regent. End of the Polish-Saxon union and of the Augustine age.

1

The King is Dead

King Augustus II 'the strong' of Poland, Elector of Saxony, died early in the morning on 1 February 1733, at the Royal Palace in Warsaw. He was affected by severe diabetes and obesity. After a fall from horse, he never recovered from an injured leg. As soon as possible after his death, the royal bedchamber, where the body was laying, was hermetically shut by order of the 'Kammerpraesident', Graf Heinrich von Brühl. The idea was to avoid leaking news and to prevent any Poles having access to the area. As soon as possible, all the secret papers and documents (including a project of partition of the Polish territories between Prussia, Saxony and Russia), the symbols of the royal power (the ring and the crown) and also the extraordinary expensive furniture were carried away and carefully stored in a cloister to prevent damage. Everything was then packed and sent to Dresden in a huge convoy of 134 carts and wagons, under escort.

Only at 7.00 p.m. did the world receive the official announcement of the King's death. The next day the bells of all the Catholic churches of Saxony announced the death of the Elector ringing for a whole hour.

The king's body, as per tradition enduring since the fifteenth century, was embalmed and remained in the Warsaw castle until 10 February. The following day the body was moved to a crypt of the Kraków's cathedral. Only the heart of the dead Elector, in a silver urn, was returned to Saxony and was deposed at the Catholic cathedral of Dresden.

The heir of the Electorate of Saxony was Friedrich August II, born in 1696. He was the only legitimate son of August. His mother was Christiane Eberhardine of Brandenburg-Bayreuth. He was groomed to succeed his father as Elector of Saxony and as King of Poland. For these reason, he converted to Catholicism in 1712. However, although he was now indisputably the new Elector of Saxony, he could not automatically succeed his father as King of Poland. August had in fact failed to make the Polish throne hereditary in his House. To save the situation Heinrich von Brühl acted rapidly.

Friedrich August II and the throne of Poland
The throne of Poland could still not be inherited. The King of Poland was elected by the *Szlachta* (the Polish nobility) in the *Sejm* (Parliament). As a result, the kings had little formal power. The *Sejm* was often paralyzed by

the so-called *Liberum Veto*, the right of any member of the *Sejm* to block its decisions. Poland's neighbors influenced the *Sejm*, and by the early eighteenth century the Polish democratic system was in decline. One of the first acts of Brühl was to raise the money to secure the election of Friedrich. The sum of 700,000 gulden out of a total of four million from the Saxon state treasury was immediately transferred to Poland.

Heinrich von Brühl was the man of the moment. Just a page at the Saxon Court in 1720, he managed to gain the favor of the King and in 1727 he was *Kammerjunker*. He met the Prinz Friedrich of Prussia at the summer military camp at Zeithain in 1730. He followed the King in Poland everywhere and, close to his master, his career progressed rapidly. Only three weeks before the king's dead he was commissioned *Kammerpraesidenten*.

On 22 February 1733, all the treasure and properties of the former King were already in the hands of the new Elector, at Dresden. Not surprisingly, considering the urgency of moment, a new career started for Count Brühl. He was also supported by the Polish Primate, Potocki. On 23 July 1733, the Count was *Kabinettsminister*. Since then the diplomat and strategist managed to gain control over Saxony and Poland partly by controlling his new master. After 1738 he was in effect sole minister, a position for which he probably had limited skills and the knowledge. Besides securing huge grants of lands for himself, he acquired numerous titles and he drew the combined salaries of these offices, amassing immense riches.

Friedrich August' interests were focused more on hunting, the opera, and the collection of artwork then on politics. Even though some portraits show him dressed in the Polish traditional costume, he would spend less than three years of his 30-year reign in Poland. The dispute started when the old enemy, Stanislaw Leszczyński, reached Warsaw in incognito. Leszczyński had been was King of Poland from 1706 until 1709. He was the great antagonist of the House of Wettin. He had been living in exile since his overthrow by August 'the Strong' after the Swedish disaster of Poltava. Returning from exile in 1733, with the help of Louis XV of France, he sparked the War of Polish Succession.

On 12 September 1733, he was elected King of Poland at Vola by a *sejm* of 13,000 supporters. As immediate reaction to this coronation, the so called 'League of the Three Black Eagles' was formed by Russia, Prussia, and Austria. The Russian army of the Empress Anna I Ivanovna (born 1693, reigned 1730–1740) started moving on September 1733. In a few weeks, 20–30,000 men under Peter von Lacy, a general of Scottish origins, put Warsaw under siege.

On 5 October 1733 at Prague, an assembly of 4,000 magnates, supporters of the Saxon Elector, elected Friedrich August II as King of Poland.

France and Spain both opposed the Austro-Russian position and supported Leszczyński. When the Russian army approached Warsaw, Leszczyński fled to Gdańsk (Danzig).

The Saxon Army on the move

Friedrich August II inherited an army that could match all the European counterparts. At the end of the Great Northern War, with the long fight against Sweden over, he had begun a reform of his armed forces. A first reorganization of the army was performed on 20 June 1717.

In 1694, the first standing Saxon Army totalled around 15,000 men (80 percent of them being foreigners). During the reign of Friedrich August I, this percentage was reduced to 28 percent. In 1730, only 11 percent of the men were not born in Saxony. The total force of the Army was by then increased to 30,000 men. The application of the 1722 Infantry Regulation and of the 1728 Cavalry Regulation was put under direct control of the Elector. The commissioning in the officer corps and NCOs was improved. In 1727 the *Invalidenkorps* was raised (two battalions, each of four companies of 166 men, 32 NCO and a staff of 21 men). The first battalion received the half-invalid men, the second battalion the full-invalid men. They served as garrison in fortresses.

Special attentions were dedicated to the dress and armament of the troops. Infantry received modern flintlocks with iron ramrod. A force of 1,200 men was stationed in Poland. The general staff was completely reformed and the country was divided in four regional Commands or *Generalate*. Four new cuirassier regiments were raised between 1730 and 1732. In the summer of 1718 near Dresden and in 1725 near Pillnitz, extensive manoeuvres of the whole army were performed under the eyes of the monarch. The troops learned to fight in three ranks in linear order. The Saxon field artillery was augmented from three to four batteries. The artillery train was raised. The summer camp of the year 1728 was totally overshadowed by the historical military event of the Parade of Zeithain, in 1730.

The financial cost of paying, re-equipping and re-arming the Saxon Army was staggering. Measures were undertaken to reduce the high desertion rate which, between 1717 and 1728, had drained 9,333 men, about a third of the army strength. The problem was reduced but, never solved. One deserter became infamous, his name was Karl Stulpner. He deserted several times during 40 years of service and after a pardon he spent ten years in the Prinz Maximilian Infantry stationed in Chemnitz before disappearing in the Bohemian forests.

The mobilization of the Saxon forces started on 6 June 1733. Two Corps were formed: the first under Archduke Johan Adolf II von Sachsen-Weissenfels with 12,800 men, the second under Count Wolf von Baudissin with 7,000 men. On 1 November 1733, a Saxon army of 18,000 men entered Poland. It was intention of the new Elector to give the command of the army to his half-brother Moritz von Sachsen, only 14 days younger than himself. 'Maurice de Saxe', as he now was called in France, was son of Aurora von Koenigsmarck, lover of the former ruler. The ambitious Maurice was in French pay and kindly refused the offer.

The War of Polish Succession

From December 1733 until March 1734 the new Saxon Elector was in Poland. On 6 January 1734, he went to Tarnowitz in Silesia to sign the *pacta convencta*. Five days later he went to Kraków, where with great pomp, on 17 January 1734, he was crowned King Augustus III at the Wawel Cathedral, by the Bishop Lipsky. J.S. Bach composed a *Cantata* for the ceremony. The army was camped around Kraków. Danzig was under siege. At the end of March 1734, the Elector was back at Dresden.

The Siege of Danzig

The allied Russian and Saxon armies besieged Danzig. The first Russian commander was Field Marshal von Münnich. He was succeeded by von Lacy. The resistance was stronger than expected. A Russian assault on 9 May against the Hangelsberg failed with great losses. The commander of the Saxon troops in Poland, von Sachsen-Weissenfels, moved eight battalions and 21 squadrons to Danzig.

On 26 May 1734, the Saxon army, camped near the suburb of Oliva in front of Danzig consisted of the following units:

> Cuirassiers: 3 sq. of Garde du Corps, 2 sq. of CR Promnitz, 2 sq. of the CR Brand, 2 sq. of CR Venediger (then Polenz), 2 sq. of the CR Prinz Gotha, 2 sq. CR Königlicher Prinz; Dragoons: (2 sq. DR Chevalier de Saxe, 2 sq. DR Schlichting (previously Goldhacker), 2 sq. of DR Leipziger (previouslly Katte), 2 sq. DR Arnstaedt;

> Infantry: 1 battalion of the *Grenadiergarde*, 2 battalions of the IR Loewendhal (previously Gotha), 1 battalion of the IR Unruh (previously Diesbach, then Marchen), 2 battalions of the IR Harthausen, 1 battalion of the IR Wilke, 1 battalion of the IR Weissenfels.

The grip on Danzig, now completely surrounded, was augmented. The Saxon regiment of the *Grenadiergarde* escorted a convoy directed to the city carrying two 48-pounder mortars and 100 bombs. The convoy crossed neutral Prussian territory. The ammunition was packed in 34 large wooden crates on eight wagons. The engineers, pontoniers, and miners pushed on the siege.

The French managed to reinforce the Danzig garrison by sea. On 23 June 1734, the fortress protecting the harbor was assaulted with the help of the Saxon heavy artillery and finally the garrison surrendered on 9 July 1734. It was not until 30 July that the city officially was in the hands of the Saxons. The cost of a six-month siege was heavy for the Russian who admitted the loss of 8,000 men. Leszczyński fled to Königsberg, in Prussia. To support him the Poles organized the Confederation of Dzików (November 1734), which, however, failed to defeat the Russians and Augustus. On 3 April 1734, 12,000 insurgents, supporters of Leszczyński, fought the last battle of the war at Kraków. They were crushed by the Saxon army and the fighting decreased all over the country. At the end of May, the Saxon army started a gradual withdrawal to Saxony. On November 1734, the new King moved to a now safer Warsaw. The hostilities were not at an end, however and from February until April 1735 small clashes continued. On 10 and 18 February, close to Konopnice, the cuirassier regiment Promnitz was attacked and, near Warta between Kalisz and Lods, so was the Chevalier de Saxe Dragoon regiment. 260 men of the foot regiment von Rochow under Major von Watzdorf were trapped by insurgents at the castle of Karge southwest of Posen on 5/6 March.

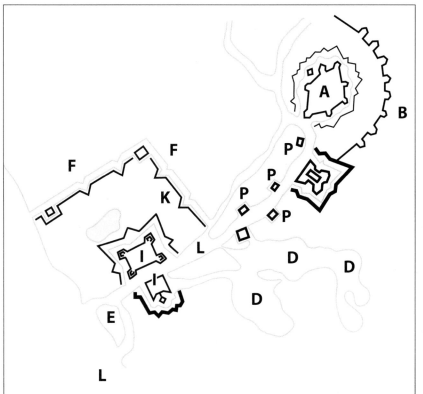

Map 1
The Siege of Danzig, after a contemporary handmade source, the map shows: A. The town of Danzig; B. The bastioned external defence line with on the left a fortified strongpoint called *Calck Schantz*; D. The flooded area known as Jasper See; P. Defensive works; L. The Baltic sea; I. The fortress of Weichsel-munde (also spelt Weixel Munde) today Wisłoujście Fortress; E. The area of the French encampment; K. The area of the French unlucky sortie; F. The Russian entrenchments.

On 7 March the Saxon force surrendered with honor and left the castle with their band playing.

The Empress Anna of Russia committed 3,000 cavalrymen against the insurgents. A mixed force of 400 Saxons and 250 Russians under General von Sybilsky fought a battle against a rebel force of 7,000. On April 1735, the fighting on the Polish soil ended. The war in Poland was over.

The Polish Succession War Outside of Poland

The war was continuing in Italy. Don Carlos, the Spanish *Infante*, led a Spanish army of 40,000 across Tuscany and the Papal States to Naples, defeated the Austrians at Bitonto on 25 May 1734, conquered Sicily, and was crowned king of Naples and Sicily as Charles III. The French, however, after overrunning Lorraine, were effectively checked in southern Germany by Austria's Prince Eugene of Savoy. Furthermore, the French and Savoyard forces that invaded Lombardy were unable to take Mantua. Tension between the Spaniards and the Savoyards made the Italian campaign of 1735 inconclusive. On another front, on June 1734, the Kaiser Karl VI asked for a Prussian allied contingent of 10,000 man. In this number were three dragoon regiments and a small unit of 60 hussars from Berlin under a young *Rittmeister* von Zieten. They joined the imperial hussars at Wiesbaden. During 1735 the fight continued to the Rhine border. A force of 6,000 Saxons was organized under *General-Lieutenant* von Friesen. The Saxon Corps consisted of six foot battalions, nine cavalry squadrons, and a company of artillery with six 3-pounders under Captain Juhr. Soon the force was put under the command of the Prince Eugene of Savoy. The Saxon force was camped near Mainz, close to the French camped at Trier.

On October 1735, the war was definitely over and France signed a preliminary peace with Austria (Peace of Vienna; 3 October 1735). Following the settlement, Leszczyński renounced the crown on 26 January 1736 and the Dzików Confederation recognized Friedrich August as King Augustus III in July 1736. On 18 November 1738, France and Austria signed the final Treaty of Vienna, in which the provisions of the preliminary agreement were confirmed and in which France also conditionally guaranteed the Pragmatic Sanction, by which Kaiser Karl VI named his daughter, the Austrian archduchess Maria Theresa, as the heiress to his Habsburg lands. The other outstanding belligerents acceded to the peace in 1739.

2

Saxon-Polish Military Activities until 1740

On June 1735, the whole Saxon army was back to the electorate. The army was divided in two *Generalate*:

1. *Generalate*: 13 battalions and 16 squadrons.
2. *Generalate*: 11 battalions and 12 squadrons.

The Leib-Grenadier Regiment and the Garde du Corps Regiment remained independent under their commanders. The Minister Brühl was commissioned *General der Infanterie* in 1734. In Poland were stationed 16 squadrons of cavalry in four regiments of light dragoons.

A corps of Saxon troops fought in Hungary from 1737 until 1739 against the Turks. This force of 8,000 men under *General-Lieutenant* Count August Joseph Sulkowsky consisted of five foot battalions and four mounted regiments, with an artillery company with eight 3-pounder guns. The Saxon Corps was directed to Belgrade across Moravia and Hungary. It fought at Timok. The campaigning was harsh but the Saxons performed quite well. On 28 September 1737, the Battle of Radojewitz was fought and lost. The company of artillery suffered heavily and two officers and several artillerymen died.

The Austrian army redeploying, the Saxons under *General-Lieutenant* Count Friedrich August Rutowsky fought a rear-guard action. At the end of 1737, out of 8,000 men only half were still under arms. The condition of the whole corps was miserable. The Chevalier de Saxe, chef of a dragoon regiment, was second in command. He wrote to a close friend at Dresden: 'We are here in a miserable condition without equipment, bread or forage. The number of sick personnel is as its high and in some companies, there are no more than ten valid men. We have no drugs nor doctors. The infantry has no tents like officers'.

The Dragoon Regiment Chevalier de Saxe left for war in Hungary in July 1737 with 398 horsemen. By the end of the year it could field only half that number. The unit lost a total of 118 men dead most of them from disease, over a quarter of its original strength. Only two years after, on January 1740, after the Peace of Belgrade, the decimated corps or what was left was sent back home.

Meanwhile the King-Elector approved some reforms affecting the Army.

- In 1734, the colour of the field uniform was changed from red to white. This would last until 1832.
- In 1736, the Military Order of Saint Heinrich was created and 21 high ranking officers received it.
- In 1737, duels were strictly forbidden.
- In 1738, some measures for children of soldiers were approved. One hundred boys and one hundred girls receive free assistance and education from the state.

As far as foreign politics were concerned, von Brühl, Prime Minister de facto since 1740 and officially since 1746, started seeking an alliance with Prussia. On 20 October 1740, the Kaiser Karl VI (born1685, reigned 1711–1740) died.

3

The First Silesian War 1740–1742

'Die Saechsische Armee war schwacht!'
'The Saxon army was weak!'

Friedrich II

Political Situation

Kaiser Karl VI, who reigned between 1711 and 1740, died on 20 October 1740. After 1711 he was the sole surviving member of the House of Habsburg. He had had no children after his marriage in 1708 and he was worried about preserving, after his death, the integrity of his vast dominions. An edict was promulgated in 1713, the so called *'Sanctio pragmatica'*. This Pragmatic Sanction stated that the vast Habsburg hereditary possessions (the Archduchy of Austria, the Kingdom of Hungary, the Kingdom of Croatia, the Kingdom of Bohemia, the Italian territories awarded to Austria by the Treaty of Utrecht – Duchy of Milan, Kingdom of Naples and of Sicily – as well as the Austrian Netherlands) could be, lacking a male heir, inherited by a daughter. Because Salic law precluded female inheritance, Karl VI needed to take this extraordinary measure to avoid a succession dispute. In 1716 a male heir was born but sadly, Leopold survived only a few months and died of smallpox. Karl's daughter Maria Theresa was born in 1717. The Pragmatic Sanction was the first such document to be publicly announced and as such required formal acceptance by the estates of the realms it concerned.

The Kaiser became obsessed by the idea of his succession and spent a lot of energy trying to secure the throne to his daughter. For years, Karl VI laboured, with the support of his closest advisor Johann Christoph von Bartenstein, to have his sanction accepted by all the courts of Europe. Only the Electorate of Saxony and the Electorate of Bavaria did not accept it, because it was detrimental to their inheritance rights. Friedrich August II, Elector of Saxony was married to Maria Josepha of Austria and Karl, Elector of Bavaria to Maria Amalia of Austria, both daughters of Charles' deceased elder brother Joseph I. According to Karl's wishes, Maria Theresa, although completely unprepared for her task, succeeded him in 1740 but the Pragmatic Sanction, instead of avoiding the risk of disputes between the European noble families, revealed itself to be the Achilles' heel of the Empire.

The Elector of Bavaria was firmly determined to claim his rights but lacked money. He found support from the powerful France of Louis XV, a long-standing archenemy of the Empire. The Bavarian army was ill prepared for war, lacking equipment and consisting of only 12,000 men: consequently, in August 1741, King Louis XV of France assembled an army of 45,000 men under the command of the Duke of Belle-Isle, between Landau and Strasbourg. Bavaria also received the support of the Elector Palatine. Piedmont and Mainz soon followed. The King-Elector of Saxony hesitated as long as possible, evaluating the situation under pressure by France. The Emperor had supported him when he was elected King of Poland, and he had militarily sustained the Emperor in the fight against the Ottoman menace. The wife of the Elector of Saxony, Maria Josepha, was an Austrian princess but he was sceptical about an involvement in a new conflict. However, the temptation to acquire more lands through in what he perceived as an easy intervention was tempting. On the other hand, he was worried by the young Prussian King, son of his former ally Friedrich Wilhelm.

On 31 March 1740, the King of Prussia Friedrich Wilhelm had died and his 28 year-old son had succeeded him as King Friedrich II (born 1712, reigned 1740–1786). Friedrich inherited an army of 90,000 men. It was the fourth strongest army in Europe after France with 203,800, Russia with 170,000, and Austria with 107,892 men. Prussia had, with a population of only 2.2 million subjects, four times the strength of the Saxon army. Out of a total of national income per year of 7 million thalers, 5.5 million were allocated to the army, almost 80 percent of the total! In comparison, Great Britain had 36,000 men under arms, Saxony 26,000 men and Bavaria 10,000 men. The recently crowned Friedrich II soon shocked Europe. Considered by most to be an intellectual, timid ruler, he claimed unexpectedly his right to some Silesian territories previously claimed by his father years before. In exchange for these lands he offered 'protection' to Maria Theresa against possible aggression. On 15 December 1740, Prussia had made an important force ready for action: 27 infantry battalions counting 20,414 men and 42 cavalry squadrons totalling 6,619 horsemen. The artillery had 42 guns with 126 artillerists. The total strength of this army amounted to 27,159 men, it was just a quarter of a perfectly equipped and drilled army. The Austrian province of Silesia was garrisoned by only 1,539 men. They were simply no match for the Prussian Army and at the end of January 1741 they started to retreat. The cities and fortresses fell one after another with poor or no resistance. Supported by France, Bavaria, and later by Saxony without any declaration of war, the Prussian army had crossed the borders of Silesia.

Mobilization of the Saxon Army

Only late in 1740 did Friedrich August II finally decide to side with Prussia, Bavaria, and France against Maria Theresa. The Saxon Army received a first order of mobilization on 28 October and a force of 20,000 men was called under arms. Count Brühl on 29 December 1740 confirmed the mobilization of the Saxon Army which was placed under Commander-in-Chief

Count Wolf von Baudissin. Saxon mobilization plans required some re-arrangements of the pre-existing units. In 1737, by merging two battalions of the Leib-Regiment with the battalion von Friesen (the former *Janitscharen*), an elite unit counting three battalions was created, the so called *Oberlaufiger Garde*. Now this unit was split again. The first two battalions formed the new IR Königin under *Oberst* von Munchow. Von Munchow was the former commander of the von Promnitz grenadier independent company in charge of the watch at the beautiful Hubertusburg Castle, attached to the Leibgarde zu Fuss. The third remaining battalion became the new IR von Schoenberg.

In 1740 the Saxon army consisted of:

1. Cavalry units: (total strength: 5,539 men and 2,050 horses):
    a. Heavy cavalry: Garde du Corps; Karabiniersgarde
    b. Cuirassier regiments: Leib-Regiment, Königlicher Prinz, Promnitz, Nassau, Prinz Gotha, Bestenbostel, Maffei, Nostitz;
    c. Dragoon regiments: Chevalier de Saxe; Arnstaedt; Schlichting; Sonderhausen

N.B.: The 2 chevauxlegers or light-dragoon regiments Prinz Karl and Sybilsky were stationed in Poland.

2. Infantry units (total strength: 13,612 infantrymen):
    Cadets 155, Engineers 43
    Grenadiergarde regiment, 1st Guards Regiment, 2nd Guards Regiment;
    Infantry Regiments Prinz Xaver, Weissenfels, Caila, Harthausen, Sulkowsky, Cosel, Römer, Allnpeck.

3. Garrison troop (total: 913 men): inwberg, 337 men; in Pleissenburg, 111 men; in Königstein, 183; Sonnenstein, 110; Stolpen, 72.

4. Militia or Reserve regiment aka *Kreisregimenter* or Circle-Regiments (total 8.000 men): four units each 2,000 men strong.

On May 1741, the army started to concentrate in the three camps of Torgau, Eilenburg and Magdeburg.

The forces in Torgau, under *General-Lieutenant* von Rutowsky, consisted of 8,644 men in 9 battalions and 10 squadrons with 9 guns and 120 artillerists.

Under GL von Jasmund,
GM von Brandt (2 sq. CR Minckwitz, 2 sq. CR Promnitz)
GM von Harthausen (2 batts IR von Cosel, 2 batts 2nd Garde)

Under GL von Bircholz
GM von Caila (2 batts IR Königin, 2 batts IR Niesemeuschel, 1 batt Grenadiergarde)
GM von Grumbkow (2 sq. DR Schlichting, 2 sq. Leib-cuirassier, 2 sq. CR Maffei cuirassiers).
9 guns with 120 men and 30 commandeered auxiliaries.

In Eilenburg, a second corps, under the Chevalier de Saxe, consisted of 11.936 infantrymen in 12 battalions and 16 squadrons of horsemen, a battalion of Grenadiergarde, Garde du Corps, Karabiniersgarde, Cuirassiers, and Dragoons, with 12 guns and 120 artillerists. The siege artillery consisted of four 24-pounder heavy guns.

Under GL von Renard

GM von Durrfeld (2 sq CR Haudring, 2 sq CR Gersdorff, 2 sq Karabiniersgarde)

GM von Rochow (2 batts IR Allnpeck, 2 batts IR Frankenberg, 2 batts IR Prinz Xaver)

Under GL von Polenz

GM von Weissbach (2 batts. 1st Guards, 2 batts IR Weissenfels, 2 batts IR von Römer)

GM von Arnim (2 sq DR Arnstaedt, 4 sq Garde du Corps,2 sq CR Königlicher Prinz)

On 4 May 1741, the Rutowsky's division left Torgau and reached Eilenburg two days later. On 18 May, the whole army paraded in front of the King-Elector. The Cuirassier Regiment Bestenbostel and the Dragoon Regiments Sonderhausen and von Pirch were left in Dresden due to the lack of mounts, waiting for horses that finally arrived in early 1742. When mounted, the dragoon regiments were posted close to the border with Poland. One battalion, seven companies strong, of the Grenadiergarde Regiment, the Independent Grenadier Company von Promnitz and the understrength Foot Regiment Sulkowsky garrisoned Dresden.

At the beginning 1741 the newly formed IR von Schoenberg (1 batt.) garrisoned the royal residences of Moritzburg, Pillnitz and Hubertusburg. At the end of May 1741, the Commander-in-Cheif von Baudissin, ordered the army back to their quarters in Torgau, Eilenburg, Meissen, Freiberg, Dresden, Zeiss, Merseburg, Lipsia, and Borna. The political situation was so indecisive and complicated that the Army, if needed (5,066 horsemen and 15,299 infantrymen) was ready to move north, towards Eilenburg or Torgau, within three days or south to Dresden within five days. In Silesia, on 10 April 1741, the Prussian army fought and won the Battle of Mollwitz (Malujowice) against the Austrians. It was the first battle of the new Prussian King Friedrich II, in which both sides made numerous military blunders but Friedrich still managed to attain victory. This battle cemented his authority over the newly conquered territory of Silesia and gave him valuable military experience.

The Saxon field artillery consisted of:

1. Staff (total 9 men): 1 commander, 1 *Major*, 1 adjutant, 1 clerk/secretary, 1 auditor, 1 *Zeugwaerterdienern*, 1 *Steckenknecht*.
2. Two companies (total 256 men) with: 2 captains or *Hauptleuten*, 2 first lieutenants, 4 second lieutenants, 2 *Stueckjunkers*, 2 *Feuerwerkscorporalen*,18 *Feuerwerken* 2 *Kanonier Sergeanten*, 2 fouriers, 2 surgeons, 8 corporals, 4 drummers, 4 fifers, 64 gunners, 128 fusiliers, 12 *Handwerfen*.

3. Regimental artillery: each Infantry Regiment had two guns served by a company officer, 1 NCO, 2 artillerists and 5 fusiliers.

Pontoniers were organised as follows:

In Saxony, a crew of 1 *Hauptmann*, 1 sergeant, 1 corporal and 6 pontoniers.
In Poland, a crew of 1 *Lieutenant* 1 sergeant, 1 corporal and 12 pontoniers
A bridge train with 20 pontoons was built in Dresden Arsenal.

The so called 'irregular' cavalry, recruited in Poland consisted of 12 mounted companies or in German *Tataren Uhlanen Hoffahnen*. Twelve *Fahnen* or flags were already on service in 1740 under *Oberst* von Bledowsky, a thirteenth company was raised on 1 January 1741, then two more followed on 1 May 1741.

State of an *Uhlanen Hoffahne* in the Spring of 1741: 1 *Rittmeister* (captain), 1 *Lieutenant*, 1 ensign, 1 kettle-drummer, each with a commoner (*Pocztowi*); 46 *Towarczys* (Polish noblemen); 46 commoners called '*pagolet*' for a total of 100 horsemen.

Each lancer was armed with a lance, sabre, a pistol, a cartridge pouch and a carbine. The lance was called '*corpikgen*', and had a typical pennant which, when waving in the wind, produced a sinister sound capable of unnerving enemy's horses. They wore a white uniform with blue as distinctive colour. In 1741, the irregular cavalry received a regulation and a set of instructions. The lancers were used to live from the country and on horseback. The *Uhlanen*, or *Tataren* as they were also called, were split in two regimental size units and were normally assigned to cover lines of communication between Saxony and Warsaw, and to the defence of the salt mine at Wieliczka in cooperation with two recently raised chevauxlegers regiments.

On 6 October, the army was in its cantonments when Rutowsky, who succeeded von Baudissin at the head of the army, gave the order to advance, in two columns, one toward Freiberg, the second toward Pirna. The order was accomplished and on 21 October the first column was quartered in the area surrounding Freiberg, Dippoldiswalde, and Frauenstein while the second column was encamped near Pirna, Fürstenwalde, and Stolpen.

In Pirna, were under Rutowsky: *General-Lieutenant* von Renard and von Polenz, *Generalmajor* von Grumbkow, von Durrfeld, von Rochow, and von Harthausen; four squadrons of Regiment Garde du Corps, two squadrons each of CR: Gersdorff, Promnitz, Minckwitz and Leib-Cuirassiers; two squadrons each of DR Schlichting and Arnstaedt (total 16 squadrons); one battalion of the Grenadiergarde and two battalions each of the 2nd Guards and of IR Prinz Xaver, Königin, Count Cosel, Niesemeuschel, and Schoenberg Fusiliers (total 13 battalions).

In Freiberg, were under the Chevalier de Saxe, *General-Lieutenant* von Bircholz, von Jasmund; *Generalmajor* von Arnim, von Weissenbach, von Caila, and von Arnstaedt: four squadrons of Karabiniersgarde, two squadrons each of CR Königlicher Prinz, Haudring and Maffei (total 10 squadrons) and two battalions each of 1st Guards and of IR Weissenfels, Allnpeck and Franckenberg (total eight battalions). Each infantry battalion had six companies (the grenadier company was added later). The Garde du Corps had four squadrons of two troops and the Karabiniersgarde had four squadrons of three troops. Cuirassier and dragoon regiments both had two squadrons of three troops.

France and Bavaria signed the Treaty of Nymphenburg on 22 May 1741, in which the French promised to support Charles Albert of Bavaria's claim to the Holy Roman Empire. Rutowsky, who was general of infantry, Governor and Commander of the Residency and of the fortresses of Königstein, Sonnenstein and Stolpen, complained about the weakness of the cavalry and of the artillery of the mobile corps. He felt deeply the lack of irregular cavalry and moreover the two chevauxlegers regiments under GL von Klingenberg were in Poland. To implement a proper artillery support, a second regimental gun was added to each battalion for a total of 21 three-pounder cannon. A further complement of four heavy siege guns was added to the artillery reserve park, these pieces were scheduled to travel by water on the Elbe river up to Lobositz or Leitmeritz (still in Austrian hands) and then by road. Two complete artillery companies were added. A supply train 'Fuhrwesen' was equipped with 500 drivers and 1,168 horses. A pontoon bridge, stored at the Dresden Arsenal, was organized with 20 pontoons.

On the March to Bohemia

The Saxon army marched on 29 October 1741. The whole army was arranged in four columns for the long march to Bohemia. The first column, acting as an avant-garde, under GL von Renard consisted of: four squadrons Karabiniersgarde, two squadrons of DR Rechenberg (former von Arnstaedt); two battalions each of 1st Guards, IR Weissenfels, and IR Frankenberg. The second column, under the direct command of Rutowsky, consisted of four squadrons of Garde du Corps; two squadrons each of CR Maffei, Leib-Cuirassiers, CR Königlicher Prinz; one battalion Grenadiergarde, two battalions each of IR Prinz Xaver and Allnpeck. Column number three under von Rochow was composed of two battalions each of IR Königin von Niesemeuschel, the *Kriegskommissariat* and the artillery. The fourth column under the Chevalier de Saxe consisted of two squadrons each of CR Promnitz, Haubring, von Minckwitz, von Gersdorff, and DR Schlichting, two battalions of the Foot Guards and two battalions of the IR von Cosel.

The field army had a post service with a *Feldpostmeister*, 1 *Postschreiber*, and *Postillonnen* with 10 horses and 6 post-wagons. The train had a bridge with 20 pontoons. In Saxony were left CR Bestenbostel, DR Sonderhausen and DR Pirch, along with IR Sulkowsky and Römer.

The first column under GL von Renard, preceding the rest of the army by five days, crossed the Bohemian border on 4 November. Leutmeritz was reached on 9 November. Along the roads posters and manifests addressed to the population were positioned to explain the intentions of the Elector of Saxony. The remaining columns crossed the Saxon-Bohemian borders on 9 November respectively at Zinnwald, Fürstenwalde, and Peterswalde; the second column proceeded to Eichwald; the third via Gehersberg and thence to Graupen and Mariascehin; the fourth via Peterswalde to Kulm and Karbitz. As predicted by Rutowsky, the march through the defiles of the mountain region slowed the manoeuvre. The weather was bad and the columns had to advance under a cold pouring rain. The Prussian army was also on the move on the Saxon left, using the recently conquered Silesian fortresses as starting points. The strong Franco-Bavarian army was moving on the Saxon right. On 13 November, the massed columns of the Saxon army reached Leitmeritz, meanwhile the first column, still acting as vanguard, had left Leitmeritz on 9 November and was marching toward Prague. Fürst Leopold von Anhalt-Dessau blocked Leitmeritz with Prussian forces leaving the Saxons free to proceed to Prague. On 15 November, the second, third, and fourth columns were on the march headed for Prague. IR Allnpeck and Schoenberg were detached to secure communications with Saxony. The siege train was slowly travelling to Prague by water, along the Elbe, up to Lobositz. On 16 November, the River Eger was crossed at three points.

The army took some needed rest in the Tursko area that was occupied 18–21 November. Patrols were sent to scout the enemy positions and contact the French. On 22 November, the Saxon army was in position near Prague, the left wing of the army reached Susdol and the right wing was close to Boromierrceliz. The French army was deployed on the Saxon left flank. The Saxon infantry was camped in the front line and the cavalry in the second line. Soon, the irregular Polish cavalry, a force of 1,200 lancers, joined the massed army. The aspect of these exotic fighters, never seen before on campaign, rapidly attracted the attention of the French soldiers. It is interesting to report a testimonial colourful description of these irregulars given by the ally: 'Most *oulans* [sic] wear no shirts. Some of them have just one and they never change it. When too dirty they wait for the clean shirt wearing their jacket on the naked skin. They eat only bread and honey. They drink just water or brandywine to fortify their stomach'. Troja, today a suburb of the capital, where the Saxon army was camped then consisted only of a small castle few kilometres north of Prague. When the field artillery arrived the work of opening a trench started.

The Storming of Prague
In 1741, the capital of Bohemia was already considered an historic site, being founded in the eighth century. The city was built across the River Vltava that flows slowly from south to north. Prague was renowned for its university and its intense intellectual activity. A 1,700 feet long, 35 feet wide, bridge with 17 arches connected the so-called *Mala Strana* or 'lesser quarter' district on the east bank with the largest part of the city on the west bank. On the west bank, the old city was limited by ancient brick walls with abandoned towers. Outside the ancient walls, the old moat has been filled when the 'New' flourishing town developed under the rule of Karl IV (1346–1378). Prague grew as a settlement stretching from the old castle called Hradčany (*Ratschin* in German) in the north and the castle of Wischehrad in the south. The Ratschin or castle area, on the east bank of the river was the oldest area. It was separated from the northern series of defensive bastions called 'the Charles Towers' just by the Royal Gardens. It is said to be the largest castle of the world at about 570 meters in length and 130 meters wide. A second castle called Vyšehrad (*Wischehrad* in German) or 'upper castle', was probably built

up around the tenth century on a hill over the Vltava river. It was located outside the bastioned enceinte and consequently had no more tactical significance. The capital city of Bohemia had also an important arsenal but in the end, could hardly sustain a regular siege. The castle area is surrounded by dominating hills and the rest of the town lays in a plain offering an easy target for artillery. The ancient brick walls were in complete disarray and almost abandoned. After the end of the Thirty Years War, when Prague was stormed during the final phase of the conflict, a line of bastions had been built all around the city by an Italian military architect in Austrian service. The works started in 1695 and were completed in the 1720.

The Franco-Bavarian army was in hurry for results and needed to take Prague immediately. The Bavarian Elector had to enter the Bohemian capital as soon as possible to be recognized a ruler. He hoped that the conquest of Prague would force the rest of the country to end hostilities. A regular siege needed time and was impossible now. The terrain was still hardened by the intense cold. Whole armies were rapidly running low of food. Inside Prague there were huge depots. A strong base of operations was also required for the next developments of a war that could be long lasting. Moreover, the Austrian army was close, the vanguards being only a few days away. On 23–24 November, the Franco-Saxon allied armies conceived a plan for a direct assault on Prague.

Brothers in Arms

Under the walls of Prague, a weird situation occurred when Moritz von Sachsen (better known as Maurice de Saxe), the half-brother of the Saxon Elector who had refused to command the Saxon army in 1733 because in he was in French pay, met the Generals Rutowsky, Johann Georg von Sachsen and *Oberst* von Cosel serving in the Saxon army. These four high rank officers were all half-brothers, all being natural sons of the former King-Elector Augustus the Strong. Maurice met his half-brothers in friendship, warmly embracing them and mentioning that, even if he was now called Maurice de Saxe, he was still their eldest brother. He took command of the risky operation. The French Commander-in-Chief, Belle-Isle, was glad to give the responsibility of the assault to his Saxon subordinate.

A four-pronged simultaneous attack was planned. The action was scheduled for the early hours of 25 November. Rutowsky had to direct his Saxons toward the series of northern bastions called the Charles Towers. Today, the only remaining part of these bastions is the so called Pisek Gate (the name is related to an old quarter of the city partly destroyed to build the bastions up) sited just a few hundred meters north of the Royal Gardens. The Pisek Gate, flanked on the left by the St. George Bastion and on the right by the Ludmille Bastion, was the only access to Prague from the north. From an aerial view, the now urbanized area of Ludmille, St. Thomas, and St. Magdalen bastions, he latter, being the closest to Vltava river, can still be recognized. The Saxon Army was camped on the right river bank around Troja.

To cross the river, the brave engineer *Oberst* von Fürstenhof (another natural son of Friedrich August I, never recognized; he died in 1753 ranked

Generalmajor as governor of the fortress of Königstein) after a reconnaissance, threw a pontoon bridge on the iced Vltava river. The bridgehead was then secured. A second Saxon attack was planned against the New Town. The French army was prepared for two more attacks. A second real attack on the New Town under the direct command of Maurice and a carefully prepared diversionary attack against the Strahover Tower, at the west end of the Old Town. The city of Prague was garrisoned by five battalions of imperial infantry supported by a militia of around 600 students and burghers, a total of around 3,000 men under General von Ogilvy. He was determined to resist until the arrival of the close by relief army under Archduke Leopold.

The Saxon assault party directed against the Charles Towers consisted of four battalions of converged grenadier companies from the foot regiments. Each grenadier battalion had a complement of 30 musicians. They were closely followed by 200 workers with shovels and pikes, torches, and lanterns. Following the storming party, as a first reserve ready to follow its advance, there were four infantry battalions consisting of musketeer companies. A second reserve of further eight battalions and 400 cavalrymen was at the ready. The attackers were under the direct command of the senior *General-Lieutenant*, Count von Renard, also General-Quartermaster of the army. A battery of 20 field guns crossed the bridge and was readied to give a fire support on the right of the attacking grenadier companies.

According to plan, on 26 November at 1.00 a.m. the French artillery, placed in front of the Strahover Tower, opened fire. The objective of the diversionary attack was to draw the attention of the garrison from the other three real attacks. To make the diversionary attack more realistic the French infantry moved from its position, approached the walls and started an intense musket fire. That night each man fired his full reserve of 60 rounds. The diversionary attack proved to be quite convincing and von Ogilvy moved his reserves from the New Town to the Old Town and the Mala Strana. However, the defenders of the Mala Strana held their position and, for this reason, the Saxons met a stiff resistance when attacking the Charles Towers. At 3.00 a.m., the Saxon grenadiers had reached their attacking position and under the bright moon light of a freezing clear night and with the help of torches and lanterns, they began the assault. They managed to cross the ditch in two points close to the Pisek Gate and to reach the wall. On the glacis, they were exposed to withering cannon and musket fire coming from the bastions. Under fire, losses piled up and when fifty men were already down the assault momentarily wavered. At the head of the attackers *Generalmajor* von Weissenbach was struck in the head by a musket ball and fell dead on the spot. The command passed to the *Oberst* von Cosel, who resumed the attack. The grenadier parties carrying ladders reached the wall and started to scale it. They finally climbed the wall and opened the gate's doors. Breaking through defences, Cosel reached the New Town crossing the bridge over the Vltava river and joined the French.

On the other side of Prague, the lucky Maurice de Saxe's attack met little or no resistance at all. The French crossed the defences without losses. The militia at first retired and then surrendered almost without resistance. *General-Lieutenant* von Renard followed through the gate with the first

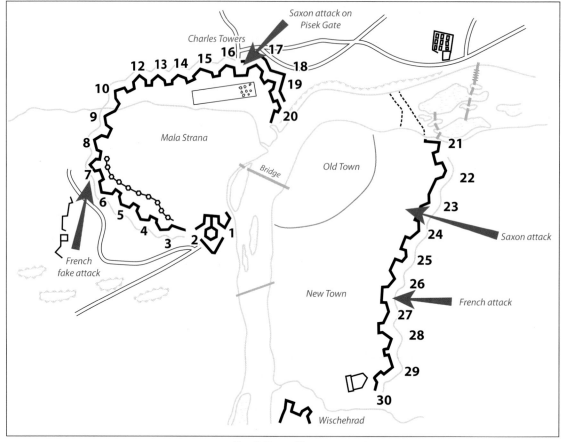

Map 2 Siege of Prague

1 Bastion St. Dominic; 2 Bastion St. Jean; 3 Bastion St. Jacques; 4 Bastion St. Charles; 5 Bastion St. Laurent; 6 Bastion St. Adelberg; 7 Bastion St. Norbert; 8 Bastion of the Hospital; 9 Bastion St. Roch; 10 Bastion St. Francis; 11 Bastion of the Star; 12 Bastion St. Mary; 13 Bastion St. Benoist; 14 Bastion St. Vincent; 15 Bastion of All Saints; 16 St. George Bastion; 17 Ludmille Bastion; 18 Bastion St. Thomas; 19 Bastion St. Magdalen; 20 Bastion St. Ignatius; 21 Bastion of the Windmill; 22 Bastion St. Christopher; 23 Bastion St. Nicolas; 24 Bastion St. Peter and St. Paul; 25 Bastion St. Henry; 26 Bastion St. Etienne; 27 Bastion St. Francis Xaver; 28 Bastion St. Bartholomew; 29 Bastion St. Catherine; 30 Bastion St. Charles; 31 The flat bastion.

reserve of four battalions and rapidly secured the walls and the main streets of Prague. Before daylight, Prague was in Saxon and French hands and the Austrian garrison had surrendered. The upper castle surrendered immediately after the town and 140 additional soldiers of the garrison were captured. At dawn the keys of the castle district were in Rutowsky's hands. The swift action left the citizens with no choice but to wait for a new master.

The total Saxon losses were three officers and 19 men dead and three officers and 40 men wounded. A total of 13 flags, 2,800 prisoners, and 300 cannon fell in the victors' hands. The prize was shared with the French army and a quarter of it was granted to the Bavarians. The Saxon battalion of the Grenadiergarde, two battalions of the Foot Guards and two battalions of IR von Cosel garrisoned the Mala Strana. IR Franckenberg and Weissenfels, under Maurice de Saxe, garrisoned the old town. The Grenadiergarde Battalion was charged with the security of the area around the palace of

Hradschin, which was occupied by the Elector of Bavaria. It was quartered in the town for several days until 29 November, when it was relieved by five fresh Bavarian battalions. During the siege, the French army was camped on the hills around Prague trying to find the best positions. The French supply corps, under the capable *Lieutenant-Général* de Sechelle supported the troops as best as possible. The cold winter took a heavy toll and already 1,000 sick soldiers crowded the field hospital. On 30 November, only the Saxon 2nd Guards were still quartered inside Prague.

On 28 November, *Oberst-Lieutenant* von Schmielinski, *aide-de-camp* of Rutowsky, was ordered to bring to Dresden the announcement of the successful assault. He praised the *Oberst-Lieutenant* Sehdens, Schlegel, Gersdorff and Carlowitz who commanded the grenadier battalions; the *Oberst* Natzmer and Franckenberg, the *Oberst-Lieutenant* Crousatz and Watzdorf who led the battalions of the first reserve; *Oberst* Cosel who descended into the ditch and scaled the walls at the head of the attackers; *General-Lieutenant* Renard who reached the gate and opened the doors; *Generalmajors* Jasmund and Rochow who headed the second attack against the New Town were delayed by the crossing of the ditch, finally entering in Prague after the French led by Maurice de Saxe. Rutowsky also commended the dead *Generalmajor* Wiessenbach, *Oberst* Neubauer, the *Oberst-Lieutenant* Schmielinski, Poniatowsky, Gersdorff, Carlowitz and Diber.

Map 3
The Theatre of War in
Bohemia

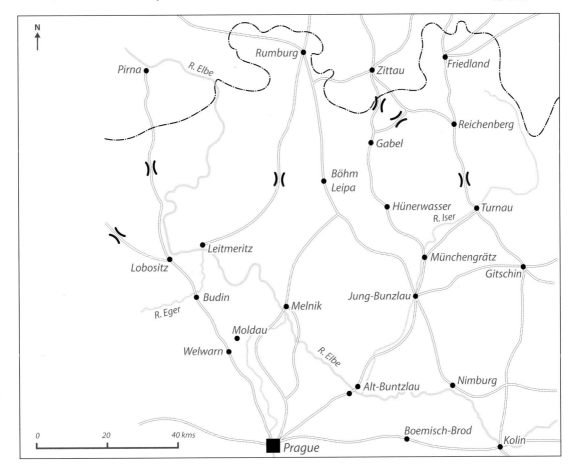

After the capture of Prague, the Allies prepared to face the Austrian army. A corps of 4,000 men under Maurice de Saxe advanced toward Kuttenberg and Kolin. A force of 800 Saxon infantrymen and three companies of uhlans managed to scout the Austrian positions around Zeleness (east of Prague). In a lucky ensuing encounter, the Polish lancers under *Oberst-Lieutenant* von Poniatowsky engaged some Austrian hussars. The Austrians, unprepared to meet the lancers, lost 60 horsemen and 47 more were taken prisoners. The Austrian position was now around Tabor behind the River Lufschniss. By 2 December, Maurice was back to Prague. The French army manoeuvred and the *Lieutenant-Général* de Polastron went toward Kamenitz and then took position behind the Sazawa River and General d'Aubigny moved toward Pilsen. The Saxon *General-Lieutenant* von Bircholz was sent to Kaurzim. The order was promptly executed and IR Prinz Xaver, Königin and Cosel, CR Königlicher Prinz and Leib-Cuirassiers with the DR Schlichtling marched towards Birchholz and reached Kaurzim on 6 December, Schwarz-Kostletz and Planian. Scouts reported that the Austrians had retired to Iglau, Pilgram, Neuhaus and Budweis. General de Polastron reached Hammerstadt and the Saxons occupied Czaslaw on 25 December. A detachment of four infantry battalion and 500 uhlans was sent toward Churdim where a cavalry force of 17 Prussian squadrons under General von Giessler, was stationed. Winter was at its height and cold intense. The French army, still under Belle-Isle and de Sechelle quartered behind the Zasawa River. Communications with Leitmeritz were secured and a depot was established there. Rutowsky's headquarters were close to Czaslaw, the *Kriegscanzlei*, the *Kasse*, and the field hospital were planned to be moved to Kolin. Austrian hussar parties caused some concern during these movements. The number of sick personnel was dramatically increasing. The army was on the move. On 19 December 1741, a force under *General-Lieutenant* von Jasmund, was directed against Deutsch-Brod when it was discovered that the town was in Austrian hands.

Encounter at Rejepin

The intense cold limited actions and the only notable episode was the so-called 'Encounter at Rejepin'. On 24 December 1741, the grenadier company of the IR Prince Xaver under *Hauptmann* Merlin was involved in a classical rear-guard action at Rejepin. The isolated company was attacked by a reconnaissance corps of 2,000 Austrian dragoons and hussars under Generals Baragay and d'Olonne. Under attack from two sides, the Saxon *Hauptmann* was able reach a castle where he found a good defensive position. A relief force under *Generalmajor* von Rochow with a battalion of IR Königin and the DR von Schlichtling managed to reach the grenadiers and to save the day. After a while, the Austrians retired with a loss of 20 dead and several wounded. The Saxons suffered two men killed in action.

By 26 December, the entire Saxon army was on the offensive. A total of 16,180 men (26 squadrons with 4,000 horsemen and 11,400 infantrymen in 19 battalions, each of approx. 600 men, and 780 uhlans) moved by Nowawes and on 29 December via Wilmow and Gothieborg, reached Przibislaw and the Austrian occupied Deutsch-Brod. *General-Lieutenant* von Jasmund attacked immediately with an infantry brigade and a cavalry brigade and took 204 prisoners and the depot. Unfortunately, the depot was almost empty. The Austrians had already moved supplies away. On 6 January, the Saxon headquarters were in Smolow. On 10 January, the army moved to Deutsch-Brod. The Saxons camped behind the Sazawa River. The Austrians had retired to Iglau and Brunn. At the beginning of January, the border of Bohemia was secure. The cold was so intense that all actions were paused.

Meanwhile, a series of defensive measures were taken in Saxony. On 7 November 1741, the irregular cavalry stationed in Poland under the command of *General-Lieutenant* von Klingenberg were authorised to cross the Brandenburg and march to Saxony. On 19 November ten companies of uhlans (a total of 722 horsemen: 30 officers, 339 nobles and 343 non-noble horsemen, 10 drummers) were at Koenigbruck from where they marched to Bohemia. The Militia regiment of Oberlaufig was activated (3rd Militia). Furthermore, a new line unit was raised, the Graf von Brühl Infantry Regiment. The staff had to be obtained from the other line infantry regiments. In 1742, the new CLR von Rutowsky was raised, its command was given to *Oberst* Vitzthum von Eckstädt. The regiment was mounted on Polish horses and had the same strength as the chevauxlegers regiments previously raised: 8 companies for a total of 753 horsemen and 722 horses. A second new infantry regiment was raised in January 1742 under Graf von Bellegarde with the same strength as the rest of the line infantry regiments.

Recruiting was now difficult and the unit remained under strength. The command of the newly raised Infantry Regiment von Brühl was given to *Oberst* von Minckwitz. During the summer of 1742 IR von Brühl camped between Friedrichstadt, Dresden and Loebtau. IR Bellegarde camped in Annaberg. Southern Saxony was only defended by the 3rd and 4th Militia regiments. On February of 1742 in anticipation of a re-opening of hostilities the field army was reinforced with the CLR Prinz Karl. This unit never reached the mobile army but was charged to secure communications.

Campaign in Moravia and Siege of Brunn

Meanwhile the French-Bavarian army was occupying Prague and the Bohemia, an Austrian army under Graf von Khevenhüller had struck deeply inside Bavaria and had reached the capital city, Munich. The course of the war had changed. The King of Prussia envisaged the occasion for a diversion and was his intention to enter Moravia, and, while blocking Iglau, to besiege Brunn. Rutowsky was seriously disappointed by the plan and during a leave personally complained with the Elector. With the Saxon army so deep in hostile Bohemia, the relatively undefended southern Saxon territories were now under a direct menace. Rutowsky obtained from Dresden only elusive answers.

The Saxon army, even if reluctantly, was forced to move to accomplish the Prussian plan.

On 5 February 1742, von Rutowsky with the Chevalier de Saxe as second in command was back to the army in Deutsch-Brod. On 9 February, the Saxon headquarter moved to Gross-Meseritsch where the army camped in two lines. On 13 February, the Prussian army was in contact with the Saxons, initially encamped in Trebitsch and then in Budischau. A Saxon detachment under *Generalmajor* von Grumbkow with five squadrons and five battalions of different regiments joined a similar Prussian detachment under *General-Lieutenant* Fürst von Anhalt-Dessau at Primlkov. The united infantry staying in Primlkov, the cavalry moved toward the Austrians in Iglau. The rest of the Saxon army followed this vanguard on 17 February and two days later was on the road to Iglau. The army was suffering from shortage of food and the humidity of the place. Rutowsky was determined to change the situation. On 7 March 1742, he left for Dresden, the command passed to the Chevalier de Saxe.

On 8 March 1742, the Saxon army was ordered by Friedrich II to put the Fortress of Brunn under formal siege. Cooperation with the Prussian army was poor. Rutowsky continued complaining about the unsatisfactory plan. Letters filled with animosity were exchanged between Dresden and Berlin.

The Saxon troops were in position around Brunn on 23 March. Five days later, the siege commenced. The Saxon force committed to Brunn consisted of:

Cavalry under GL von Bircholz

GM von Arnim 2 sq. CR von Minckwitz, 2 sq. CR von Gersdorff, 1 sq. CR O'Byrn

GM von Durrfeld 2 sq. CR Maffei, 2 sq. CR Königlicher Prinz

Infantry under GL von Jasmund

GM von Rochow 2 battalions of IR Cosel, 2 of IR Prince Xaver, 2 of IR Niesemeuschel

GM von Caila 2 battalions of IR Frankenberg, 2 of IR Schoenberg, 2 of IR Weissenfels 1 batt of the Grenadiergarde

The determined garrison of Brunn reacted. A party of four battalions and four squadrons from the defenders of Brunn and 500 Austrian hussars attacked the besieging troops. An entire squadron of DR von Rechenberg was caught by surprise in the open while foraging and was captured.

In the French army, Belle-Isle reassumed command from de Broglie and initiated the siege of Eger. The French Army was now facing an Austrian army of 40,000 men under Prinz Karl von Löthringen. Belle-Isle formally requested Saxon assistance and on 5 April 1742, King Friedrich of Prussia decided to call off the siege of Brunn. On 7 April 1742, *Feldmarschall* Johann Adolf II von Sachsen-Weissenfels took command of the Saxon army.

On 15 April four companies of IR Cosel acting as vanguard, under *Oberst* von Sedenz who was killed, were ambushed by the Austrians disguised as workers and suffered severe losses in dead, wounded and prisoners. Four regimental guns and four flags fell into Austrian hands.

The Saxons under the interim command of the Chevalier de Saxe left from Brunn in four columns, reached northern Bohemia, and camped between Leitmeritz and Schlachenwerth on the northern bank of the Eger. The strong position was fortified with earthworks and fleches and provided with obstacles (the so-called 'Spanish horses'). The infantry camped in the first line camped and the cavalry camped behind them. The regimental guns were in position close to their parental units. The heavy artillery was stored at

Leitmeritz. The whole army was split in two wings, the first under Rutowsky, who had returned to the army, the second under the Chevalier de Saxe. In the middle camped the chevauxlegers and the uhlans with responsibility for patrolling and security. Stable communications between the army and the homeland were assured. In such position, the army could resist a long time.

Weissenfels sent back to Saxony two squadrons of Garde du Corps, and the badly reduced DR Rechenberg and IR Cosel for rest and refit. Five new companies of uhlans under *Oberst* Schchodinsky reached the army.

On 25 June, *Feldmarschall* von Weissenfels received the order to stop actions against the Austrians and prepare to repatriate the army. On 28 June 1742, the Peace of Berlin between Prussia and Austria was signed. Only few days after, the Saxon army received the order to retreat and in four columns they moved back to Bohemia from Brunn via Oels.

The official end of the First Silesian War was signed in Berlin, on 28 June 1742. Maria Theresa ceded most of Silesia with the County of Kladsko to Friedrich, except for those districts of the Duchy of Troppau that were located south of the Opava river, including the southern part of the former Duchy of Jägerndorf, the possession of which had been one pretext for Friedrich's invasion. The Duchy of Neisse held by the Breslau bishops was also partitioned, with the fortress-city of Nysa and the larger northern portion of the territory falling to Prussia. Austria retained the entire Upper Silesian Duchy of Teschen, ruled by Maria Theresa's husband, Francis. Prussia in turn left the anti-Habsburg coalition it had forged with France, Spain, Sweden, Naples and the Electorates of Bavaria, Saxony and Cologne.

4

The Second Silesian War 1744–1745

Situation of the Saxon Army at the end of 1742

In September 1742, the Saxon army was organized in two distinct military districts (*Generalate*) encamped near Dresden (first *Generalate* under Rutowsky) and Chemnitz (second *Generalate* under Chevalier de Saxe). Dresden was garrisoned by IR Brühl, the Garde du Corps and the Grenadiergarde Regiment all belonging to the first *Generalate*. The mobile army counted 14,458 men in 16 squadrons, 12 battalions, two companies of artillery with 300 artillerists, and 171 men of the train.

Rutowsky was in command. The whole army included 8,000 militiamen or *Kreistruppen* at the end of 1742 and reached 45,323 men, with 8,493 horsemen with 8,010 horses and 1,276 artillerists. The infantry consisted of the Grenadiergarde and 15 infantry regiments, each counting 1,657 men for a total of 26,803 men. The fortresses of Wittenberg, Pleissenburg, Königstein, Sonnenstein and Stolpen were garrisoned by 852 men. The four Kreisregiments at 1,975 men each, totalled 7,900 men.

The Strange War

Prussia resumed hostilities on 10 August 1744, the so-called *Präventivkrieg* (Preventative War). Between 14 August and 2 September 1744, 60,000 Prussians marched across Saxony. Around 600 boats were directed on the Elbe from Torgau, via Meissen, Pirna, Lobositz, and Budin to Prague. The 4,000-man garrison of the Bohemian capital city capitulated on 16 September. The city's stores of ammunitions, equipment and food were captured. 130 guns, 9,000 flintlocks and 2,500 uniforms fell in Prussian hands. The city paid 1.3 million gulden. The Saxon army was completely surprised by the Prussian action. The army did not react against the ex-ally and remained quartered in their cantonments.

On 2 October 1744, finally mobilized, the mobile army concentrated at Adorf, under the command of von Sachsen-Weissenfels, and started moving towards Bohemia. The Chevalier de Saxe was second in command and the army was organized into two corps.

First Corps
GL von Polenz
GM von Schlichting: 2 sq. CR Bestenbostel, 2 sq. CR Königlicher Prinz, 2 sq. DR
    Sonderhausen
GL von Renard
GM von Harthausen: 2 batts. 1st Guards, 1 batt. IR Königin, 1 batt. IR Weissenfels
GM Neubauer: 2 batts. IR Gotha, 1 batt. IR Brühl, 2 batts IR Prinz Xaver, 1 batt.
    2nd Guards
GL von Bircholz
GM von Durrfeld: 2 sq. DR Schlichting, 4 sq. Karabiniersgarde

Second Corps
GL von Jasmund
GM von Schlichting: 2 sq. CR Gersdorff, 2 sq. CR Haudring
GM von Wilster: 1 batt. IR Schonberg, 1 batt. IR von Pirch, 1 batt. IR von Römer
GM von Frankenberg: 1 batt. IR Cosel, 1 batt. IR Allnpeck, 1 batt. IR
    Niesemeuschel
GM von Durrfeld: 2 sq. CR Maffei, 2 sq. CR O'Byrn

Each battalion had 2 regimental guns. The four artillery companies received a complement of 50 additional men. An independent unit of 20 *Feldjägers* was raised.

The homeland was defended by General von Bose with 16 infantry battalions and 16 cavalry squadrons. These troops were divided in two Corps:

First Corps under Gen. Graf von Rutowsky
GL von Arnim, GM von Arnstaedt and von Cosel: 4 sq. Garde du Corps, 4 sq.
    CLR Rutowsky, 2 sq. CR Minckwitz, 2 batts. Leibgrenadiergarde, 1 batt. 2nd
    Guards, 1 batt IR Königin, 1 batt. IR von Pirch, 1 batt. IR von Brühl, 1 batt IR
    von Cosel, 1 batt. IR Bellegarde

Second Corps under Gen. von Diemar
GL von Grumbkow, GM von Rochow, von Grosse, and von Minckwitz: 2 sq.
    Leib-Cuirassiers, 2 sq. DR von Pirch, 2 sq. DR von Rechenberg, 1 batt. IR
    von Weissenfels, 1 batt. IR von Römer, 1 batt. IR Allnpeck, 1 batt. IR von
    Niesemeuschel, 1 batt. IR Schoenberg, 2 batt. IR von Stolberg

The total of the forces in Saxony was 3,169 horsemen and 13,504 infantrymen plus the 4 *Kreisregiments* of militia.

On 4 October, the mobile army set off in two columns. On 13 October Pilsen was reached. On 21 and 22 the Moldova river was crossed on two pontoon bridges and a floating bridge at Zebrut Wester. On 24 the Saxons effected a junction with the Austrian army which consisted of 30 cavalry regiments and 71 battalions under *Feldmarschall* Prinz Karl von Löthringen. On 31 October, the allied army was near Trebeschitz. The Saxon vanguard consisted of 20 companies of uhlans and 10 companies of grenadiers.

The Prussian army concentrated on the right bank of the Elbe river close to Kolin and Pardubitz were they had provisions. On 19 November, the enemy was close and was attacked at Teltshitz (now Chvaletice) on the Elbe. The Bohemian people started armed resistance against the Prussians. With its lines of communication cut and no more food and supplies, the Prussian army started to heavily suffer from desertion. At first the Prussian army decided to resist in Prague then a crucial decision was made, to retreat from Prague to Silesia. To retreat in the cold Bohemian winter was a dangerous action. The total cost of the retreat for Prussians was staggering. In total, the Prussian army lost around 30,000 men. Around 15,000 men deserted (9,000 between 26 November and 4 December). Along the roads, 5,000 dead were left. The Austrians only captured 3,200 prisoners. Out of 17,000 Prussian soldiers leaving Prague only 2,000 reached the Silesian border. In Prague 164 guns were left (the captured guns and other 34 Prussian guns), and all the baggage. All without a single battle.

On 1 December, the advancing Saxon uhlans captured 400 Prussian hussars. On 4 December, 15 hussars and 2 officers were captured along with some wagons with the loss of 3 dead and 6 wounded. During the winter 1744/45 the King of Prussia started a series of measures to compensate for the losses suffered in the previous campaign. France sent a subsidy of 3 million thalers. Five hundred retired officers were recalled. A general pardon was granted for deserters. A premium was given for enrolling but despite all these efforts by April 1745 units were still incomplete.

On 8 January 1745, the alliance between Saxony, Austria, the Britain, and the Dutch Republic was signed at Warsaw. According to the Treaty of Warsaw, Saxony received £150,000 in return for agreeing to field an army of 30,000 against France and Prussia. This brought Saxony into intimate relations with Britain for the first time. Within months all signatories had formed an alliance against France. On 20 January 1745 Kaiser Karl VII died and his son, the Elector Maximilian III Joseph of Bavaria signed, on 22 April at Fussen, peace with Austria. These events dramatically changed the balance of power in Germany, and the allies were ultimately successful in securing recognition for Maria Theresa at the Treaty of Aix-la-Chapelle.

With the arrival of the spring of 1745 Prussia resumed operations. Consequently, as agreed at Warsaw, Saxony was forced to field a fighting force of 30,000 men. To defend Saxony, there were just six squadrons, five battalions and an artillery company with 10 pieces, positioned between Leipzig and Merseburg under *General-Lieutenant* von Arnim. The main Saxon army marched towards Silesia

On 9 May the Saxon vanguard effected a junction with Nádasdy's troops. The joint armies then advanced in five columns. The Saxon were in the fifth. On 26 May Weissenfels assumed the overall command.

On 29 May, 25,121 men in 18 battalions and 24 squadrons with 52 guns (8 six-pounders, 4 twelve-pounders, and four 24-pounder howitzers) were at Landeshut (Kamienna Gora). On 1 June, they reached Guntersdorf. The Prussians were posted southeast of Schweidnitz (Swidnica) between Frankenstein (Zabkowice Slovakia) and Neisse (Nysa) close to Glatz (Klodzko). The concentration was planned for 22 May, at Frankenstein. With the Saxons there were also some Austrian horse regiments: Karl Pálffy, Lucchesi, Czernim and Birchenfeld for a total of 28 squadrons.

The Battle of Hohenfriedeberg

On 3 June at 4.00 a.m., the united Austro-Saxon army advanced in eight columns from Striegau (Strzegom). The commander-in-chief of the allied army was Prinz Karl von Löthringen. Beside him was *Feldmarschall* Johann Adolph II von Sachsen-Weissenfels with the Saxon contingent of 22,530 men: 18 infantry battalions, 18 grenadier companies, four squadrons of the Karabiniersgarde, four squadrons of chevauxlegers, 12 squadrons of cuirassiers, four squadrons of dragoons and 22 companies of *uhlans*. Rutowsky was second in command and the Chevalier de Saxe was in command of the cavalry. Together, the two armies numbered over 40,000 infantrymen and 18,300 horsemen with 121 guns (81 regimental guns and 40 heavy guns).

Against them the slightly inferior in number Prussian army had 38,600 infantrymen and 19,900 horsemen with 192 guns (138 regimental and 54 heavy). The Prussian King was in command. The army moved in the darkness of the early morning of 4 June. Friedrich launched a surprise attack on the Saxon camp. The Prussians then concentrated their efforts against the Austrians whose cavalry was rapidly driven out the field. After a fierce resistance, the Austrian infantry finally broke when the Bayreuth Dragoons charged through a gap in the Austrian lines. The battle ended with the complete defeat of the Austro-Saxon army.

After the battle, 4,018 dead were collected by friend and foe and put in mass graves.

The Saxon losses at Hohenfriedberg were severe. All of the generals were wounded, some died. The roll call after the battle gave just 16,685 men and 4,385 horses. The cavalry lost eight officers and 545 horsemen, the infantry 20 officers, 1,874 men and 976 wounded. The total losses were 3,423 men, 805 horses and all 66 guns.

In mid-August 1745, to face the critical situation, 12,000 Saxons were recalled to their homeland and only 6,000 men remained with the Austrians. Two columns moved respectively on 26 and 29 August: the first, under von Bircholz, consisted of eight squadrons and six battalions, the second, under von Renard consisted of eight squadrons, six battalions, the artillery park, and the commissariat. On 15 September, the men paraded at Dresden in front of the King-Elector. It was then directed to a camp in the area of Ubingen where it stayed for some days, Only 6,000 men remained with the Austrians.

On 22 August, the army camp was moved closer to Leipzig between Gholis and Schonfeld. The whole army was, finally, reunited on September in a new camp, close to Lipsia, between the small villages of Mockau and Gohlis.

On 10 October Rutowsky camped in a new location near Seehausen and Gutritsch and on the 14th the army paraded in front of the King-Elector.

Between 26 and 28 October new cantonments were decided. They allowed for the entire army to concentrate within 72 hours. They were organised in 3 *Generalate*:

1. Von Diemar at Merseburg
2. Von Renard at Lipsia
3. Von Bircholz at Eilenburg

Generalmajor von Sybilsky with light troops (chevauxlegers and uhlans) patrolled a cordon between Baffendorf and Landsberg.

The Battle of Soor

The 6,000 Saxons still campaigning with the Austrian army were involved in the Battle of Soor. Prinz Karl von Löthringen once more commanded the Austro-Saxon army. He tried to surprise the Prussians in their camp but scouts detected the advance of his army and sounded the alarm, thus allowing the Prussian army to deploy before the attack. The Prussian cavalry routed the Austrian cavalry but was forced to withdraw when it came under musket fire. The Prussian infantry then launched a first assault which was repulsed. Finally, an unplanned attack by a few Prussian battalions decided the day. In this battle, the Saxon lost 27 dead and 474 wounded.

The Battle of Kesselsdorf

On 29 November 1745, Leopold I von Anhalt-Dessau was in command of a Prussian invasion corps of 24,577 men. This force consisting of 28 battalions, 63 squadrons and 32 guns entered into Saxony, while a second Prussian corps of 30,000 under the direct command of the King of Prussia was in Königsbrück supporting the attack of the old general. In a few days, 'the Old Dessauer' reached Lipsia. The city was plundered and two million thalers were exacted. During this time, the Saxon army was marching in the direction of Silesia to combine with the Austrian forces against Friedrich's corps. The strategic situation changed abruptly and now Saxony itself was in danger.

Lipsia was already in Prussian hands when the 43-years-old Rutowsky replaced Sachsen-Weissenfels as commander-in-chief of the Saxon army. The enemy was approaching and one after another the cities and the fortresses of Saxony were surrendering. The military depots in Torgau and Meissen were already lost. The bridge at Meissen on the Elbe was left intact and the Prussians were left free to cross the natural obstacle and march on Dresden. The Saxon army converged on Kesselsdorf on 14 December 1745. Situated five kilometres east of Dresden, this was a conveniently defensive position (which has not changed since these days and can today be reached by the B173 road). To boost the morale of the troops, soldiers received half a month of pay.

The defenders had 31,000 men: 24,000 foot and 7,000 horsemen with 42 heavy guns. This included an Austrian contingent of 6,370 men under *Feldmarschall-Leutnant* Graf von Grünne. Prinz Karl von Löthringen with an additional 20,000 men, was not far away, near the Dresden Great Gardens area, but his men never reached the battlefield. The temperature was low in the cold continental winter and troops received little or no food. The battlefield was a quite open and rolling plain suitable for cavalry charges. Terrain was hard and frozen and the soil was covered by a thin coat of snow.

The right flank was turned into a strong fortified position. Pioneers and engineers had erected a series of gun batteries. Twenty guns were in position on the west of the village. A battery of six guns covered the west access. Two other batteries, one of eight guns and one of 12 guns, were on the western outskirt. The elite of the Saxon army consisting of seven grenadier battalions was positioned inside Kesselsdorf. From the village to the right flank, the rest of the army deployed in a line seven kilometres long.

On 15 December at 7.30 a.m. the Prussians advanced. Four advancing columns of attack, 21,000 infantrymen and 9,000 horsemen with 33 guns, closed in on Kesselsdorf from Wilsdruff and struck the Saxons. The commander, 'the Old Dessauer' was the true architect of the Prussian army. Under his command was probably the most disciplined and best-drilled infantry of Europe. Battalions were perfectly able to march at steady speed to close with the enemy. Against this well-known formidable war machine stood the whole Saxon army under Graf von Rutowsky. He was aware of the adversary as a former student of 'the Old Dessauer', having served in the Prussian army as a colonel 17 years before.

At 2.00 p.m., the Saxon artillery opened fire on the left starting the battle. Six grenadier battalions attacked the most exposed Saxon battery. They were supported by two cavalry regiment and 14 guns under *General-Lieutenant* von Wilster. The guns roared, firing canister at the enemy, and the defenders opened musketry fire when the grenadiers were at 60–70 paces. The dust covered the attackers. The assault failed and the Prussian battalions broke under fire. The last battle of 'the Old Dessauer' seemed to be a failure but the old general remained determined to defeat the Saxons. The Prussians marched on the crunching snow. This second attack directed on Kesselsdorf failed, as the first one, in a dark cloud of black smoke. At this point the victory at his hand, Rutowsky probably made a mistake. Anxious to close the day he decided to face the Prussian army in the open.

The Saxon IR von Pirch, after sustaining two consecutive Prussian assaults at severe cost, was exhausted. The Prussians had almost reached the church of Kesselsdorf when they were repelled, the defenders losing a flag in the process. The regiment from Chemnitz, IR Niesemeuschel, clashed against the Prussians but they remained unbroken. The Prussians continued their attack until a large part of Kesselsdorf was in their hands but at the end they were repelled.

Two Saxon grenadier battalions then left their defensive position and attacked in open field. Two Prussian guns were already lost when 'the Old Dessauer', seeing the Saxon right flank uncovered by its counter-attack, ordered an all-out attack. Two regiments kept in reserve charged the infantry in the open. The Prussian infantry resisted, and, supported by the cavalry, counter-attacked. The Saxon infantry, under pressure from all sides, broke. The fleeing troops were driven back into Kesselsdorf and the Prussians seized the heavy battery. The Prussian left wing then advanced to attack the centre of the Saxon line. Disordered by the loss of Kesselsdorf, the line was wavering. Bloody hand-to-hand fighting ensued with bayonets and swords. The Saxons panicked and the whole line crumbled down and started a disorderly retreat. At 16.30 the battle was lost and the Saxons beaten. The soldiers surrendered or were in full retreat. The Austrian troops on the Saxon extreme right maintained their position for a while then retreated. The troops under Prinz Karl camping in the Great Garden in the southern outskirts of Dresden were still uncommitted.

On the field were laying 10,000 dead and wounded men of both armies intermixed with hundreds of bodies of dead horses. The chances of surviving for a wounded man were very small and most of them died during the ensuing night. Hundreds of wounded horses were wandering around the battlefield without riders. It started snowing and soon the whole battlefield was covered. No help could come from Kesselsdorf whose inhabitants had left before the battle. Only a flock of plunderers coming from the nearby villages started searching the bodies.

The Prussians had lost a total 135 officers and 4,901 soldiers (4,759 were infantrymen). This represented one sixth of their total strength. They had captured eight flags. The Saxon army lost in two hours of battle one general, two colonels, one major and 54 other officers, 3,752 NCOs and other ranks plus 727 horses. The IR Niesemeuschel suffered particularly badly. Around 3,000 men and 141 officers were captured. The artillery lost 48 guns, 187 men and 249 horses. The total losses of the Saxon army were estimated close to a third of its total strength.

The Rutowsky left with his retreating army, reaching the Great Garden where the Austrians were camped. The Austrians retired via Gross-Sedlitz and Dippoldiswalde, crossed the Bohemian border and reached their winterquarters. Friedrich August II and Graf von Brühl had already on 1 December reached Prague. The Saxon capital surrendered two days later.

The commander in Dresden was the old General Adam Heinrich von Bose. A force of 12,000 Prussians camped in the town and 2,000 wounded were attended. Every single soldier received a pound of meat, two pounds of bread and two pints of beer per day. An officer received 5 thalers per day. In ten days, the city gave 90,000 thalers-worth of food to the Prussian army.

One day after the capitulation was signed, Friedrich entered Dresden accompanied by four infantry regiments. The King slept in the Rutowsky's Palace and requested 1 million thalers. Out of 3,000 militiamen present in Dresden he took 1,600 into Prussian service along with 26 cadets. The prisoners of war were set free. The garrison was forced to lay down the arms in the Old Market Place, on 18 December and left the town.

The Austrian army fell back to the Bohemian border. On Christmas day, the Saxons agreed to pay 1 million thalers as reparation and the Peace of Dresden was signed. The Second Silesian War was over. The Austrians had to acknowledge Friedrich as legitimate sovereign of Silesia and Glatz. Friedrich recognized the husband of Maria Theresa, Franz Stephan von Löthringen, as Kaiser with the name of Franz I.

Nothing changed for Austria, Saxony was the loser and the role of this country as an independent power had come to an end. Prussia was raised to the rank of a major European power. Within two weeks the Prussian army left Dresden and Saxony. On 27 December Friedrich II left Dresden and the next day he arrived in Berlin where he was received in triumph.

Aftermath

Total loss of the Saxon army in the various campaigns of 1745 amounted to eight colonels, four staff officers, 110 officers, 6,209 men and 1,772 horses.

On January 1746, Friedrich August II left Prague for Dresden. Under General von Polenz a force of six battalions and 18 squadrons remained in Bohemia as an auxiliary corps. The rest returned to Saxony again.

The following peace lasted for ten years. In May 1746 Sachsen-Weissenfels died and Rutowsky succeeded him. The Saxon army was severely reduced during the following years.

- In 1746 nine cavalry regiments were disbanded.
- In 1748 four infantry regiments were disbanded.
- In 1749 268 officers were pensioned.
- In 1750 the strength of each company was reduced by 1 officer and 20 men.

In 1753 this reduced army paraded in front of Rutowsky at the summer camp in Ubingen. The same year the Army consisted of 15,015 men and 5,032 horsemen. The total strength, including the four militia *Kreisregiments*, amounted to 26,826 men and 4,408 horses. Soon afterwards the *Kreisregiments* were disbanded and only a cadre for each was retained. A cavalry regiment had 514 troopers and 393 horses and an infantry regiments had 1,104 men. The infantry regiment Niesemeuschel of Chemnitz received a new Chef in 1753. It was the three-year-old Prinz Friedrich August, later Elector Friedrich August III and King Friedrich August I of Saxony. The regiment name changed to IR Prinz Friedrich August. In 1754 the four *Generalate* were reduced to only two. There were two independent units: the Garde du Corps under the Chevalier de Saxe and the Leibgrenadiergarde under Graf von Rutowsky at Dresden.

Graf von Brühl commanded in Poland with the rank of *General der Infanterie*. Under him were the elite cavalry regiment of Karabiniersgardes, three chevaulegers regiments, and three Uhlan *pulks* for a total of 16 squadrons, and 24 irregular companies totalling 3,771 horsemen and 2,643 horses.

5

Saxon Cavalry in the Seven Years War

In October 1756, as will be related in the second volume of this work, the main Saxon army capitulated near Pirna. Virtually the entire Saxon army ceased to exist. The men were pressed in Prussian service. All but four regiments were disbanded. Four Saxon cavalry regiments and two irregular Polish Uhlan *pulks* garrisoned at that time around Kraków survived. The cavalry corps was under *Generalmajor* Georg Ludwig, Graf Nostitz and consisted of:

> Karabinier regiment (*Generalmajor* Wolf Kaspar von Zezschwitz, 533 horsemen)
> CLR1 Prinz Karl (*Oberst-Lieutenant* Benkendorff, 766 horsemen)
> CLR2 Graf Brühl (*Oberst* von Gößnitz, 766 horsemen)
> CLR3 Prinz Albrecht (*Generalmajor* von Monro, 542 horsemen)
> Uhlan *Pulk* Rudnicki (426 horsemen)
> Uhlan *Pulk* Renard (426 horsemen)

Immediately after the arrival of Augustus III in Warsaw, negotiations started with the court in Vienna about the use of these regiments beside the Austrian army. An agreement with Maria Theresa was reached and the units moved on 15 November 1756 from Kraków to Hungary. The winter quarters were in Komitates Neutra and Trentschin (present day Nitra and Trentschin, Slovakia).

The Karabiniersgarde and CLR Prinz Karl were the first to join the Austrian army under *Feldmarschall* Leopold Daun. On 8 May 1757, they reached the main army camped south of Olmütz (present day Olomouoc, Slovakia). On 15 May arrived CLR Prinz Albrecht and CLR Brühl under command of *Generalmajor* von Monro. All four regiments were allocated to Graf von Nádasdy's vanguard camped at Maleschau, south of Kolin.

On 14 June, the three regiments were involved in a skirmish near Kuttenberg (present day Kutna Hora, Czech Republic) losing 20 men.

The Saxon chevaux-legers regiments distinguished in the attack against the Prussians during the Battle of Kolin on 18 June 1757. The Prussian von Rochow Cuirassiers were driven back by the CLR Brühl and Prinz Karl, the Prussian von Kyau Cuirassiers by the CLR Prinz Albrecht. This last unit followed the Prussian cavalry and captured 900 prisoners while the two others attacked the Prussian infantry. CLR Brühl captured four guns and eight flags. Four were left in the hands of the Captain von Kracht. Four squadrons of CLR Prinz Karl annihilated the Prussian Grenadier Battalion von Waldau. Two other Prussian regiments were routed, the Prinz Heinrich and von Munchow. The Prussians lost 45 pieces of artillery and 21 flags and standards. The Austrian cavalry under Graf von Starhemberg pursued the Prussians afterwards. The Saxon Karabiniersgarde were part of the reserve and mounted later with the Austrian cavalry regiments Alt-Württemberg, Starkenfels, and Savoyen.

The total losses of the Saxon regiments at Kolin were 53 dead, 116 wounded. 177 horses also died and 85 were wounded. *Generalmajor* von Nostitz, at the end of the battle sent his adjutant, *Lieutenant* Freund, to August III at Warsaw with the message about the great victory. *Generalmajor* von Nostitz was promoted to *General-Lieutenant*, *Oberst* von Gößnitz to *Generalmajor*, *Oberst-Lieutenant* von Benkendorff to *Oberst* and *Rittmeister* Kracht to *Major*. The success of the Saxon regiment obscured the action of the irregular *pulks*. They followed with other light troops the retreating Prussian army after the battle. The outcome of the battle of Kolin was of far-reaching political, moral, and symbolic importance.

The vanguard left the day after. The main army remained on the battlefield. The Saxon chevaux-legers regiments of Nádasdy's corps followed the Prussians to Leitmeritz. The bridge had been burned by the enemy. The Prussians were on the right bank of the Elbe. The Saxons crossed by swimming and reached on 25 July, Tetschen (present day Decin, Czech Republic). From there Nádasdy turned toward Rumburg and at the end of August to the main army in the region of Herwigsdorf, near Zittau.

Nádasdy, on 7 September 1757 routed near Moys (present day Zgorzelec, Poland) the Prussian *General-Lieutenant* Winterfeld's isolated corps. The Saxon Karabiniersgarde, with the Duke of Aremberg's Reserve Corps, joined in battle the three chevaux-legers regiments.

At the end of September, 96 Karabiniersgardes under *Rittmeister* Johann Gottlieb von Bulow took part in the *Feldmarschall-Leutnant* Hadik's raid to Berlin.

The first of the Austrians to arrive before Schweidnitz (present day Swidnica, Poland) were those of Nádasdy's corps (including the three Saxon chevaux-legers regiments), who placed it under blockade on 30 September. A contingent from Württemberg and the Austrian Corps de Reserve brought the besiegers to a strength of 43,000. On 24 October, the place was sealed. Schweidnitz surrendered on 12 November 1757.

Upper Lusatia remained occupied by troops of *Feldzeugmeister* Ernst Marschall von Burgholzhaisen. The Karabiniersgarde under *Generalmajor* von Zezschwitz were with these troops.

After capitulation of Schweidnitz, Nádasdy joined the main Austrian army and on 22 October participated on the Battle of Breslau (present day Wroclaw, Poland). During the battle the Saxon chevaux-legers clashed against the Prussian cuirassiers. *Oberst* Benkendorff with CLR Prinz Karl was again distinguished.

On 5 December, the Saxon chevaux-legers fought at Leuthen (present day Lutynia, Poland). CLR Prinz Albrecht fought against the Prussian cavalry that routed the Württemberg and Bavarian infantry. During the battle the *General-Lieutenant* von Nostitz was severely wounded and taken prisoner. He died of his wounds on 7 January 1758. The Saxon losses were 418 men and 423 horses.

The Karabiniersgarde and both the Uhlan *pulks* spent the winter near Welwarn (present day Velvary, Czech Republic) and moved, on 11 January 1758 to Raudnitz (present day Roudnice).

The 3 chevaux-legers regiments after Leuthen were directed to Moravia, with headquarters at Sternberg (present day Sternberk, Czech Republic). The interim commander was *Generalmajor* von Monro. After the death of von Nostitz, *Generalmajor* von Monro was promoted *General-Lieutenant* and was in command of all the four cavalry regiments. In April, when the Karabiniersgarde and the Uhlan *pulks* went also moved to Moravia, the Saxon cavalry regiments were again united.

When the Prussians entered Moravia, the Saxon cavalry was in the corps of *Feldmarschall-Leutnant* de Ville. The Uhlan *pulks* distinguished themselves in the so called *Kleiner Krieg* ('little war').

In June CLR Prinz Karl and Uhlan *Pulk* Rudnicki were at Prerau under *Generalmajor* St. Ignon. On 17 June, they attacked Holitz and Gross Wisternitz.

On 29 June The Prussians drove the Uhlan *Pulk* Renard out from Kralitz to Klenowitze (present day Kralice na Hané, Czech Republic) but at night the Uhlans counterattacked successfully.

On 30 June CLR Prinz Karl and the Rudnicki Uhlans participated in the capture of a large Prussian convoy at Domstadtl. The Prussian stopped the siege of Olmütz. The Saxon cavalry with the St. Ignon corps followed the retreating Prussians. Later they were sent to Moravia again and in July they camped near Troppau (present day Opava, Czech Republic). De Ville rallied with *Feldzeugmeister* Harsch's corps. Neisse was besieged (present day Nysa, Poland) but the bad weather caused the siege to be raised and the army went to winter quarters. The Saxons camped to Moravia-Silesia border near Troppau and Teschen.

At the beginning of 1759 the Uhlan *pulks* were at 602 men each, the four cavalry regiments at 807–813 men. Prinz Karl in 1758 obtained the title Duke of Kurland and so his chevaux-legers regiment changed designation and was called 'Kurland'.

On 17 April 1759 de Ville's corps was massed near Heidenplitsch (present day Bilcice, Czech Republic and went to a camp between Troppau and Jägerndorf (present day Opava and Krnov, Czech Republic). The corps was sent in July to Bohemia against General von Wedell who has occupied Trautenau (present day Trutnov, Czech Republic). De Ville moved with Harsch's corps to Silesia. The Saxons under *Generalmajor* von Zezschwitz acted as vanguard.

The camp at Grusau abby (present day Krzeszow, Poland) was attacked on 18 July by the Prussians under Fouqué but the enemy was driven back. After some skirmishes the corps returned to Trautenau, de Ville went to

Saxony and the Saxon cavalry remained with the Harsch's corps. At the end of November 1759 *Feldmarschall* Daun called the Saxon cavalry to Saxony. One column with CLR Prinz Albrecht and the Karabiniersgarde moved from Trautenau via Schlukenau (present day Sluknov, Czech Republic) and Neustadt, a second column with the others moved via Reichenberg (present day Liberec, Czech Republic) and Zittau. The Rudniki Uhlans moved from Brunn (present day Brno, Czech Republic). The Uhlan *Pulk* Schiebel (former Renard) had already arrived. All the regiment spent part of the winter near Stolpen/Saxony. On 15 January 1760, they moved again toward the Silesian border. The Prussian army was in position at Gorlitz.

On 1 April 1760 both the uhlan *pulks* were reinforced to 1,000 men each. The whole Saxon cavalry corps counted now 5,288 men and was assigned to the corps of *Feldzeugmeister* Franz Moritz Lacy near Radeberg. The uhlans camped near Strehla, the chevaux-legers at Königsbrück. On 1 June, *Generalmajor* von Zezschwitz with a mixed Austro-Saxon force attacked by surprise Kossdorf occupied by four squadrons of Prussian hussars and 4 officers and 69 hussars were captured.

In September, for the second time in the war, the Austrians could deal a blow against Berlin. The town was a centre of administration and together with Potsdam it housed manufactures and stores of weapons and military equipment. In October 1760 Lacy was delighted to receive an independent command. He had under his command 17 battalions, 17 companies of grenadiers, one company of jägers, 50 squadrons of horse, and a train of 63 pieces of artillery: in all, 18,500 men. Lacy had more man than the force which Hadik had brought against Berlin in 1757, but this time the Austrian were operating in support of the Russian allies, which proved to be more complicated than expected. The CLR Prinz Albrecht and Brühl and both the Uhlan *pulks* were in the number. Under *Generalfeldwachtmeister* Emmerich Esterhazy, together with the Austrian HR Kaiser, the Uhlans reached Potsdam. The regiments requisitioned military clothing in the *Montirungskammer* and wrecked as much as they could of the celebrated small arms factory of the *Splitgerber und Daum* combine. The men broke up the weapons, tools and lathes and threw the brassware into the Havel along with more than 18,000 musket locks. The two other regiments under the command of *Feldmarschall-Leutnant* Buttler followed in support. By 11 October Lacy had news from Daun. Lacy rode on to the Elbe from where the sound of artillery had been heard on 14 October. He moved his corps to Plossing on 17 October. The exhausted men could enjoy some rest.

The blow at Berlin contributed to breaking the stalemate in Silesia, and drew Friedrich and Daun over to the west. Friedrich and his army were on the march. It was a general move of the main Prussian forces. The Austrian moved to the Elbe river and the enemies clashed at the bloody Battle of Torgau, fought on 3 November 1760. On that day, Lacy's corps and the Saxon corps confronted 18,000 Prussians under von Zieten. The Austrian army was beaten. The Saxon cavalry supported the Austrian light troops and suffered from the heavy Prussian artillery fire. Immediately after the battle the Austrians divided their forces. The main army passed the Elbe dismantling the three boat bridges behind it. The corps of Lacy retired up the west bank of the river and covered the most direct road to Dresden. Lacy's corps bivouacked every night in the open air, for the train of tents had been sent across the Elbe with the rest of the Austrian baggage. The corps marched without stopping to reach Strehla on 4 November. On 8 November, the corps fell back to the vicinity of Dresden.

General-Lieutenant Wolf Kaspar von Zezschwitz went in January 1761 to Vienna and on the way of return stopped for some days at Prague. On 9 March 1761, he suffered a stroke and died. *Generalmajor* Wolf Heinrich von Gößnitz was promoted *General-Lieutenant*. The Saxon cavalry remained the whole year in Saxony, without great action. Winter camps were placed around Chemnitz, later near Penig.

On 5 January 1762 CLR Prinz Albrecht and Brühl, under *Generalmajor* Renard with two Austrian cavalry regiments and two infantry regiments under *Generalmajor* Sulkowsky were sent to Altemburg.

The Karabiniersgarde, CLR Prinz Karl and the Schiebel Uhlans participated on the raid of Graf von Lobkowitz against the Prussians near Audigast and Groitsch. Later the Saxon cavalry corps was allocated to Maquire's corps near Dippoldiswalde. At the end of June, the Saxons were on the Saxon-Bohemian border. During a surprise attack by troops of *Generalmajor* von Kleist at Boemisch Einsiedel (present day Mnisek, Czech Republic) on 2 July 100 light horsemen and Karabiniersgarde were captured by the Prussian. *General-Lieutenant* von Gößnitz reported that the horses of the detachment were too fatigued after 14 days without food, and not suited for an escape.

General de Cavalerie Andreas Graf von Hadik took the command of the Austrian army in Saxony and drove the troops of *Generalmajor* von Kleist from Freiberg on 29 October 1762. General Buttler with 2,000 men in action out of his 8,000 men, supported the attack. Some volunteers of the CLR Prinz Albrecht under *Lieutenant* von Rex cleared the Mulde valley of Prussian jägers. *Oberst* Schiebel with his *pulk* occupied Hilbersdorf. CLR Prinz Albrecht and Schiebel Uhlans captured one Prussian twelve-pounder gun. During the battle the Prussian losses were 5,000–6,000 men. Foggy weather helped the Prussian retreat. The peace depended in part on retaining the corner of Saxony around Dresden.

On 4 November Hadik was forced to report that the Reichsarmee had retreated from Frauenstein to Altenberg close to the border ridge with Bohemia. At the end of this campaign the hard circumstances of service and the bad financial situation (soldiers were not paid for months) resulted in a very bad shape of the Saxon cavalry. The uniforms were tattered, the soldiers fatigued. Since November 1762 the regiments camped around Fischbach, the headquarters of *General-Lieutenant* von Gößnitz was at Puzkau.

On 17 November, the Prussian army was still on the offensive on another front. *Generalmajor* von Kleist struck from Chemnitz with 6,000 troops and invaded Franconia. He proceeded to exact contributions from Bamberg, Furth, Erlangen, the Bisphoric of Fulda, and the Principality of Meiningen. He did not care to meet the contingents of Saxon troops which were returning from service with the French and so he turned about with the great train of cash, hostages and, plunder, and reached Lipsia by way of Erfurt on 8 December. The last shots of the Seven Years War on the continent of Europe were probably fired at this time, just as the first had been discharged at Stolpen.

On 24 November Hadik concluded a winter truce with the enemy. The talks between Maria Theresa and Friedrich opened on 30 December and extended through January 1763. At the beginning of February Friedrich wrote 'we agree on everything. The treaty of peace will be signed next week'. The preliminary of the Peace of Hubertusburg were signed on 15 February.

In the spring of 1763 the Saxon cavalry regiments returned home and met the infantry already returned from French service. The Seven Years War was over.

6

General Staff, Adjutants, and Headquarters Troops

Since the beginning of the Saxon standing army, at the head of the army there was a *Feldmarschall*. The *Feldmarschall* was also called *General en Chef*. He was the commander-in-chief but was conditioned by the will of the Elector and of his Minister of War. He was responsible for strategy. It is interesting to note how, when *Feldmarschall* Sachsen-Weissenfels died in 1746, in a moment of deep crisis, for several years the rank of *Feldmarschall* was left vacant until Graf von Rutowsky succeeded to the post.

Under the *Feldmarschall* the other general ranks were as follows. The general of service (that is to say, of infantry or of cavalry) or in German *General der Waffengattung* was an intermediate rank, commonly referred as 'General', between the *Feldmarschall* and the *General-Lieutenant*. A *General-Lieutenant* was in command of up to six regiments. A *Generalmajor* was in command of up to three regiments, an ad-hoc formation, or a group of battalions. They were on charge of the tactical employment of troops in combat and of the exact execution of orders. The general headquarters of the Saxon Army was in Dresden like the *Feldmarschall* and the general staff.

The country was divided in several military areas called *Generalate*. The number of the *Generalate*, during the period considered varied for economy reasons from four to only two. In 1730, the four commands were respectively in Wittenberg (I), Zeitz (II), Freiberg (III) and Dahme (IV). Generals von Bose,[1] Graf Wolf von Baudissin, von Mickau, and Sachsen-Weissenfels,[2] were in command. Each zone had also a *General-Lieutenant* and two *Generalmajors*.

---

1   Adam Heinrich von Bose, was born on 3 March 1667 in Unterfrankleben. He died on 21 May 1749 in Moelbis. *General der Infanterie* and governor of the city and the Fortress of Wittemberg, Knight of the Military Order of St. Heinrich. He signed in Dresden the Capitulation of 1745.

2   Johann Adolf II von Sachsen-Weissenfels was born on 4 September 1685 in Weissenfels. He died on 16 March 1746 in Lipsia. He served in the Hessian army during the Spanish Succession War then, following his father, entered the Saxon service in 1711. He served as *Generalmajor* and fought in the Battle of Straslund during the Great Northern War. In 1723, he was made *General der Kavallerie*. In 1733, he fought in Poland with Burkhard Christoph von Münnich at the Siege of Danzig. He commanded the troops in Poland until 1736. He was made a Knight of the Military Order of St. Heinrich in 1736.

In 1730 the whole General Staff consisted of a total of 25 officers:

- 1 *Feldmarschall*: Field-Marshal Graf von Wackerbarth
- 2 *Generale der Kavallerie* (Generals of the Cavalry)
- 1 *General der Infanterie* (General of the Infantry)
- 5 *General-Lieutenant der Kavallerie* (lieutenant generals of cavalry)
- 3 *General-Lieutenant der Infanterie* (lieutenant generals of infantry)
- 1 *General-Lieutenant der Ingenieure* (lieutenant general of engineers)
- 6 *Generalmajore der Kavallerie* (major generals of cavalry)
- 4 *Generalmajore der Infanterie* (major generals of infantry)
- 1 *Generalmajor der Artillerie* (major general of artillery)
- 1 *Generalmajor des Zeugwesen* (major-general of the train)

To the general staff were added:

- 1 *Inspekteur der Kavallerie*
- 1 *Inspekteur der Infanterie*
- 1 *Exercitienmaister der Kavallerie*
- 1 *Exercitienmaister der Infanterie*

In 1733, when August the Strong died the structure of the *Generalate* changed only in details. The number of generals increased with time (see Appendix I: Saxon General Staff 1733). Generals served for life but were granted leave or retirement for health reasons.

In 1740, the 20,000 men strong Saxon Army was under the command of:

9 *Generale*: von Baudissin, von Kiefenwetter, von Bose, von St. Paul, Graf von Sulkowsky, von Zuhlen, Graf von Rutowsky, Graf von Castell and Chevalier de Saxe;

13 *General-Lieutenants*: von Brass, von Bodt, Fürst Lubomirsky, von Kavanagh, von Pfugk, von Diemar, von Bircholz, Graf Lubomirsky, von Klingenberg, von Renard, the Prinz von Holstein, von Polenz, von Jasmund;

20 *Generalmajore*: von Riedesel, von Marchen, von Diesbach, von Haugwitz, the Prince von Gotha, von Grosse, von Goldacker, von Grumbkow, Brand von Lindau, von Arnim, von Sibilski, von Zembeck, von la Sarre, von Unruh, von Rochow, von Weissbach, von Caila, von Durrfeld, von Harthausen, von Fürstenhof (general-quartermaster). For a complete list of the officers see Appendix II Saxon Staff 1740.

At the head of the army was the *Kriegsrathkollegium* (College of the War Council).

In September 1742, the Saxon army was organized in two distinct *Generalate* encamped near Dresden (first *Generalate* under Rutowsky) and Chemnitz (second *Generalate* under the Chevalier de Saxe).

Between 1743 and 1750, in Saxony, there were a total of 36 squadrons and 32 battalions. The Army – under the command of *Feldmarschall* Sachsen-Weissenfels and the Inspectors, respectively of the cavalry *Generalmajor* von Durrfeld, and of the infantry *Generalmajor* von Rochow – was divided into four *Generalate*.

I *Generalate*: Gen. von Bose at Wittenberg. GL von Bircholz, GM von Arnstaedt and Graf von Cosel at Torgau.

Cavalry: DR Schlichting, 2 sq. at Luckau; DR Pirch 2 sq.at Grimma; DR Rechenberg, 2 sq.at Presch; Leib-Cuirassiers, 2 sq. at Oschass

Infantry: 2nd Guards at Hertzberg; IR Graf von Cosel at Torgau; IR Graf von Brühl at Lubben; IR Frankenberg at Lipsia.

II *Generalate*: Gen. Graf von Rutowsky at Dresden (Governor), GL von Jasmund and GM von Arnim at Bautzen.

Cavalry: CLR Rutowsky 4 sq. at Grossenhain; CR von Minckwitz, 2 sq at Camenz; CR O'Byrn, 2 sq. at Muskau.

Infantry: Leibgrenadiergarde at Dresden; IR Königin at Gorlitz; IR Sulkowsky at Bautzen; IR Bellegarde at Dobeln.

III *Generalate*: Gen. Chevalier de Saxe at Dresden. GL von Polenz, GM von Grumbkow and GM von Caila at Chemnitz.

Cavalry: Garde du Korps, 4 sq. at Dresden; CR Maffei 2 sq.at Freiberg; CR Bestenbostel, 2 sq. at Weida; CR Gersdorff, 2 sq. at Reichenbach.

Infantry: IR Römer at Zwickau; IR Allnpeck at Schneeberg; IR Niesemeuschel at Freiberg; IR Schoenberg at Chemnitz.

IV *Generalate*: Gen. von Diemar; GL Graf von Renard; GM Graf von Brühl and GM von Harthausen at Naumburg;

Cavalry: DR Prinz Sonderhausen, 2 sq. at Colleda; Karabiniersgarde, 4 sq. at Zeiss; CR Königlicher Prinz, 2 sq. at Merseburg; CR Haudring, 2 sq. at Sangerhausen;

Infantry: 1st Guards at Borna, IR Prinz Xaver at Naumburg, IR Weissenfels at Langensalza, IR Stolberg at Eisleben.

Poland was garrisoned by GM von Sybilsky with 4 sq. of CLR Prinz Karl, 4 sq. CLR von Sybilsky, and 23 companies of Uhlans.

After Kesselsdorf command was given once more to *Feldmarschall* Sachsen-Weissenfels. There were still four military regions or divisions: the *Generalate* of Naumburg, Torgau, Freiberg, and Zwickau. In the summer of 1746 the *Generalate* were commonly referred from the headquarters location (for example Torgau or Naumburg, etc.). The Ingenieurs Korps was divided in two brigades. The *Auditeurs* were ranked as *Lieutenants*. In 1744, the *Feldwachtreglement* was approved, consisting in a field-manual concerning the order of march of the army in campaign for both cavalry and infantry. Also, the activity of priests on campaign was regulated.

In 1754 the four *Generalate* were reduced to only two:

I Torgau: *Kommandeur, General der Kavallerie* von Arnim (16 squadrons and 12 battalions) with 8,843 men and 1,674 horses.

II Naumburg: *Kommandeur, General der Infanterie* von Rochow (12 squadrons and 11 battalions) with 8,278 men and 1,179 horses.

Rutowsky complained with reduction of the strength of the Saxon Army but with no avail.

Uniform of Generals

At the beginning of the 18th century, the uniforms of the general officers of the European armies remained un-regulated. A first attempt to regulate the aspect of the high-ranking officers was made in France in 1724, where a coat of civilian derivation in the colours of the Royal House was adopted. The nobility received the new coat very coldly. Then Spain followed, adopting exactly the same items, with a better acceptance. Saxony was among the first of the European states to follow them, even if unofficially. The Saxon generals wore, in the field, a plain coat of dark red velvet, of the same cut of the rest of the army. An example of this uniform is shown in the portrait of General Jean de Bodt, dated 1729, by Louis de Silvestre. Other portraits of general officers still in existence demonstrate that a common uniform was accepted. On parade, the rank was distinguishable by the amount of gold embroideries on the front, cuffs, and turnbacks of the coat.

The generals could optionally wear a cuirass in the field and on parade (both a black enamelled and a white polished one) with golden fittings. The general's buttons were gold, as was the feathered tricorne edge, except for the Elector Friedrich August II who had a silver-laced uniform. Generals could wear riding boots (*Stiefel*) or gaiters (*Gamaschen*). Generals of artillery had a green coat faced red. Officers wore a sash (the oldest officer's rank distinction) around the waist. The loose part of this sash (*Trageweise*) could be left hanging on the right or the left side of the body, indifferently. The horse furniture saddlecloth (*Schabracke*) and cover of the pistol holster (*Schabruncke*) of generals were edged in gold.

On 7 March 1735, according to a general order (*Allerhoechte Entschliessung*), the whole general staff received their first officially regulated uniform. A full dress (*Paradeuniform*) and a service dress (*Interimsuniform*) were prescribed for all the ranks. The field of the single breasted coat was white, as for the rest of the army, with large dark red cuffs and turnbacks. The rank of the general was evident from the decoration of the coat and of the red waist coat, which became richer the higher the rank.

The general officers who were also proprietors of a regiment *(Inhaber)* also wore the uniform of their unit.

The white coat was worn until 1752 when, on 29 November 29, a new uniform for generals was prescribed. This new uniform was officially adopted on 10 February 1753. The field colour of the coat was changed again in a dark shade of red known as *Ponceau Rot*. It was the same colour as the Leibgrenadiergarde's coat. The facing colour was of the same red. The general ranks were distinguished by a double lace of a larger and a thinner gold lace on the front of the coat, around the horizontal pockets, around the handcuffs edges for a *General-Lieutenant* (following the French style of time '*à la Bourgogne*'). For a *Generalmajor*, a single thinner gold lace edging the front of the coat, the pockets and handcuffs was prescribed. The collar of the coat was edged by a single gold lace, larger for a *General-Lieutenant* and thinner for *Generalmajor*. The waistcoat was now of a straw colour with gold embroidered lace according to the rank. The headgear was a cocked hat edged in golden lace, festooned for *General en Chef*. All generals hat had white feathering.

The cuirass on field service was no longer in use until 1759, when a precise order on the matter, issued in Warsaw, reached the Saxon Corps in French pay, reintroducing it as a protection measure after the death in combat of the *General-Lieutenant* von Dyherrn. This order required that the cuirass should be worn under the coat and over the waistcoat when on mounted service.

Jägerkorps

A diminutive unit closely related to the staff was the Saxon *Jägerkorps*. The personnel, in German *Jägers* (literally 'hunters') was formed, as in other countries, of chosen men recruited from gamekeepers and hunters. The personnel, limited in number to the strength of a cavalry squadron, could operate on foot or mounted. They were equipped as cavalrymen but better armed, receiving the expensive rifled carbine. The men were instructed to act as military police, mounted guides, messengers and escort for high-ranking officers. Information about this unit, including its date or raising, are scarce.

We luckily know their uniform in 1744 from a plate, of the former De Ridder Collection now in the Bibliothèque nationale, by an unknown artist probably copied at the end of the 19th or beginning of the 20th century by the German artist Trache. This shows that the *Jägers* wore a grey coat of the same cut of the rest of the army with green facing on collar, lapels, cuffs, and turnbacks. The edges of collar, cuffs, turnbacks, and buttonholes were silver laced. The button were in white metal. On the right shoulder, there was an *aiguillette*. The breeches were made of light yellow wool or of deerskin left in the natural color. For mounted service high boots were used, otherwise socks and gaiters over black shoes. The black cocked hat had silver lace and a silver button with white cockade. The horse equipment consisted of a green saddlecloth and green pistol covers with white edging.

Frei-Husaren von Schill, or Leibjäger

Another small cavalry unit, closely related to the previous one, often barely mentioned, also deserves some attention. The unit was the Volunteers Hussars of von Schill also known as *Leibjäger*.

In 1761, Johann Georg von Schill was serving as volunteer with some hussars in the Reichsarmee. He was the father of Ferdinand von Schill, the major of the Prussian army who, in 1809, revolted against the French and was killed at the Battle of Straslund. Prinz Xaver, commander of the the10,000 Saxons in French pay, accepted the offer of von Schill to join with his hussars.

Von Schill was able to increase the strength of his small unit to 100 men and was promoted captain (*Rittmeister*) in the Saxon Army.

On campaign, this single squadron served as Life Guard for Prinz Xaver (also known in the French army as Comte de Lusace). This unit co-operated with and included a number of Jägers. They were raised for similar tasks as the Fusiliers-Guides serving with the French General Staff. At the end of the Seven Years War, the squadron was incorporated into the re-raised Freiherr von Sacken Light Dragoons (former Graf Rutowsky Light Dragoons).

As for the Jägers, information about this small unit are limited but the *Gazette van Ghendt* reports that, on 27 August 1762, *Rittmeister* Schill assaulted a Brunswick party in the Erfurt area, killing some, taking prisoner a lieutenant and 26 men along with 30 horses.

In October 1762, mounted Jägers and hussars under the command of von Schill were to be found near Gotha. On 4 November 1762, Schill, operating with the Austrian Ottosche Jägers surprised some Prussian troops in Weißensee (some 8 km NW of Sömmerda in Thuringia) and succeeded in breaking down the town gates. They took prisoners some 30 Prussians prisoner and got 40 packhorses and baggage as booty.

On 20 November 1762, Schill with hussars and mounted jägers surprised another small detachment of Brunswick Hussars and *Türken*. The enemy party under the command of a captain had been forcefully collecting cattle in the Fulda and Würtzburg areas and had acquired some 100 head. The captain and some 20 of his men were taken prisoners, as were 30 horses. Schill then had the cattle returned to their original owners. The location of this skirmish is given as 'Yhrsprünge'; this may be 'Urspring', part of Pretzfeld in Oberfranken.

The Volunteers Hussars' uniform was inspired by the Austrian Hungarian light cavalry dress. Our sources for this uniform are an old plate by R. Trache (the German illustrator active before WWI), copied later by Schirmer 1989 and Friedrich 1998; and another plate by unknown author in De Ridder collection kept at the Bibliothèque Nationale de France in Paris.

The headgear was a red mirliton with a black flame edged white normally wound around the mirliton with a white over red plume. The dolman was yellow with white lace and white facing on collar and cuffs. The pelisse was white with red lace and white metal buttons. The breeches were red with white Hungarian knots and lace. The Hungarian low boots had a white lace and tassel. The sabretache had a red field edged by a white braid with two yellow stripes and was embellished with the Royal 'AR' cipher surmounted by a crown. The pointed saddlecloth had a white field with a red vandyked stripe in the Hungarian style.

7

Adeliges Kadettenkorps (*Corps des Cadets-gentilhommes*)

In 1687, under the rule of Elector Johann Georg III, an order signed by von Bose, coming from the General Headquarters in Dresden, provided 6,000 *Rixthalers* from the *Kriegkasse*, for the education of 60 young nobles for a period of one year. The officer in charge of the first company of cadets was *Oberst* Klengel. In 1692, a class of cadets was officially established for the first time. Its initial organization comprised a staff of 5 officers (Prima plana) and a class of 30 noble cadets. In 1693 and 1694, a detachment of cadets accompanied the Saxon Army during its campaigns on the Rhine. In 1699, the registers of the War Ministry indicated the existence of companies containing 124 noble cadets.

In 1725, the *Militär-Akademie* was established, by order of the *Feldmarschall*, Graf von Wackerbarth, and divided into two distinct companies: the *Ritter-Akademie* and the *Militär-Akademie*. In the summer of the same year, the whole corps camped near Pillnitz.

In 1730, the Institution was renamed 'Corps'. From the *Kompanie zu Pferd* (mounted company) originated the *Grand Mousquetiers* (in existence 1730–1735). The same year, the corps camped in Zeithain and paraded in front of the King of Prussia.

At the time of the Seven Years War, the unit had the following *Chefs*:

- from 1748: Kurprinz Friedrich Christian
- from 1763: The Elector of Saxony

Throughout its history, the unit had the following captains:

- from 1691: *Feldmarschall* von Schoening (died in 1696 at the age of 55)
- from 1696: *General-Lieutenant* von Bircholz (promoted *General der Infanterie* and Governor of Dresden in 1697)
- from 1701: *Generalfeldzeugmeister* Graf von Zinzendorf (also Governor of Dresden, resigned as *Feldmarschall*)
- from 1712: *General der Kavallerie* Janus Chevalier von Eberstadt (also Governor of Dresden)

- from 1718: *General der Infanterie* Graf von Wackerbarth (also Governor of Dresden, died as *Feldmarschall*)
- from 1738: *Generalmajor* von Minckwitz
- from 1746: *Oberst* von Sternstein (then commander of a *Kreisregiment*)
- from 1748 to 1756: *Oberst* von Pahlen (died as *Generalmajor* in 1760)
- from 1763: the new Corps was under command of *Generalmajor* von Benningsen (later *General Inspecteur, General-Lieutenant*, resigned and was proprietor of a regiment of the line)

Throughout its history, the unit had the following captain-lieutenants:

- from 1692: von Bose, then *General der Infanterie* and Governor of Wittenberg
- from 1694: von Gersdorff
- from 1695: *Major* von Schöning
- from 1697: *Hauptmann* von Wirkholz
- from 1700: *Hauptmann* von Seydlitz
- from 1701: *Hauptmann* von Seynitz
- from 1712: *Oberst* von Pflugg
- from 1719: *Oberst* Baron Bothmar
- from 1725: *Oberst* Baron Rochow
- from 1733: *Oberst* von Arnim
- from 1734: *Oberst* von Minckwitz
- from 1738: *Oberst-Lieutenant* von Sternstein
- from 1740: *Oberst-Lieutenant* von Pahlen
- from 1744: *Major* von Sternstein
- from 1752 to 1756: *Oberst-Lieutenant* von Benningsen
- from 1763: the new unit was commanded by the *Oberst-Lieutenant* von Plötz (died as *Oberst*)

In 1756, during the Prussian invasion of Saxony, all Cadets were captured by the Prussian Army on the heights around Pirna and forced to surrender like the rest of the Saxon Army. Even when the Elector of Saxony asked personally to Friedrich II for the permission to be accompanied in his exile in Poland by the young nobles he was humiliated once more. Only eight cadets of Polish origin were left free to reach their families. A new corps was raised in 1763.

The Uniforms of Cadets

In 1695, the cadets received the same uniform recently adopted by the Saxon Army, a plain dark red coat or *justaucorps*. The seeking for uniformity is shown by the presence in the staff of each 12-company infantry regiment of 12 tailors deputed to provide right fittings coats and breeches to each unit.

In 1730, the Corps, reviewed at the summer camp of Zeithain, wore the red uniform faced white with silver buttons and laces. The Corps uniform remained constantly red also when the rest of the army was dressed in white. Only the cut of the coat was renewed, following the fashion.

The manuscript of the *Deutsches Historisches Museum* (DHM) in Berlin shows two uniforms in 1756: a service dress and a Gala uniform.

The service dress consisted of a plain red with a collarless coat faced red. Also red were the waistcoat and the breeches. A black felt tricorne laced white with cockade, white belt and gaiters (black/dark grey in winter and white in summer) on black shoes completed the dress.

On parade, the cadets wore a much more expensive red coat with a low collar faced white, with white lapels edged silver, with 8 white metal buttons and 8 silver laced buttonholes arranged 2-2-2-2 on each lapel. The cuffs were also white edged silver, each with 3 white metal buttons and 3 silver laced buttonholes. Turnbacks were white and were kept fastened in place with a white metal button. A silver *aiguillette* was hanging from the right shoulder.

The waistcoat was white edged in silver with horizontal pockets and white metal buttons and silver laced buttonholes.

The breeches were white. The gaiters, worn over black shoes, were of white fabric.

8

Swiss Lifeguards (*Schweizerleibgarde*)

The *Fusstrabanten* or Foot Guards (the term *Trabant*, plural –*ten*, was used in Sweden, to indicate a guard on foot armed with halberd) of the Saxon Elector had a long history. Their title changed during the ages several times. A small unit of 20 men entitled *Oberguardia* was raised in 1555. In 1569 the unit was reinforced up to 58 men. This number was doubled up to 112 men in 1669 but later reduced by half, for economy, in 1670.

In the following years, the strength of the *Trabanten* remained relatively unchanged.

The *Trabanten-Leibgarde zu Fuss* (Foot Bodyguard) changed name on 24 May 1725 after a royal order (the elector was at that time King of Poland).

Augustus the Strong was an admirer of King Louis XIV and consequently the Saxon *Trabanten* were re-modelled after the French *Cent-Suisses* aka as the 'Hundred-Swiss', the personal Swiss Bodyguards of the French King. The unit was entitled *Schweizerleibgarde* (Swiss Bodyguard). At the meantime, the rank of the commander of the unit, the *Trabanten-Hauptmann* (captain of the trabanten) was changed to *Schweizer-Hauptmann* (swiss-captain).

The first officer appointed as *Schweizer-Hauptmann* was a Frenchman native to the Beaujolais, his name was Pierre Brohenques. He entered the Saxon service after a period spent in French service. He moved to Warsaw on 24 May 1726 and married Mademoiselle de Barques, an illegitimate daughter of the elector. Then in 1725, he visited Paris for the marriage of Louis XV to the Saxon Princess Maria Leszczyńska.

The *Schweizerleibgarde* was not only entrusted with the security of the royal family but were also in charge of the surveillance of the Dresden palace and of the inestimable treasures it contained.

The captain was deputed to the strict control of the unit. He had to visit periodically the watch posts in person or throughout subaltern officers. None was admitted, without permission, inside the royal palace and, most of all, into the royal apartments. The Guards had to check for perfect order inside each apartment and to refer to the civil deputies about eventual problems. The captain was responsible for the discipline and for the selected recruitment of the unit. However, he had no power to dismiss anyone of the personnel without the consent and permission of the elector himself or, in his absence, of the grand-marshal.

The captain was the keeper of the keys of the palace. He had to take the keys with him every day and he could pass them to a subaltern officer on service only at the time of the closing of the doors. He could never leave the palace without a written permission nor without leaving a substitute. The unit was also in charge of the early warning in case of fire. The danger of a fire in a structure built mainly of wood was a real one. In 1701, a fire destroyed a large part of the *Residenzschloss* or Residence, the *Georgenbau*, which was soon rebuilt in Baroque style by Augustus the Strong. The *Langer Gang*, a long arcaded open structure connecting the *Johanneum* with the *Georgenbau*, was also repaired. In case of fire, the guards were to alert their superiors and the elector himself. They should be able to refer carefully about the ongoing problem and be prepared to receive orders. To protect the safety of the Elector, the *Schweizerleibgarde* had to be always ready to refer about every unusual event happening inside the palace. To accomplish his duty, the effective strength of the corps was augmented. By an express order of the elector, the personnel had to be of Swiss nationality, good complexion and high stature. The recruitment of the Swiss encountered some difficulties and a mission was sent to Switzerland, at first to the St-Gallen Canton and then to Bern and Fribourg. In a letter, the king-elector explained that he was indifferent about the exact provenience of the personnel but, the unit had to be completed for the autumn of 1730. The sum of 1,200 thalers from the *Generalkriegskasse* was granted to the administration of the unit for the raising this same unit. The sum included 126 thalers for two NCOs as assistants to the captain (the newly introduced rank was entitled archer).

Under the *Schweizer-Hauptmann*, the General-Adjutant von Diesebach was appointed as captain-lieutenant and the Graf von Cronhielm was appointed as lieutenant. The staff received, in addition, a sub-lieutenant and an ensign. The officers of the *Schweizerleibgarde* had a superior rank in respect of the army equivalent. Consequently, the *Schweizer-Hauptmann* was a *Generalmajor*; the captain-lieutenant had the rank of *Oberst*; the lieutenant, the rank of *Oberst-Lieutenant*; the sub-lieutenant was a *Major*; and the ensign had the rank of a captain of the line.

On 1 January 1730, the unit consisted of:

- 1 captain
- 1 captain-lieutenant
- 1 lieutenant
- 1 sub-lieutenant
- 1 ensign
- 1 secretary
- 1 *wachtmeister*-lieutenant
- 1 *porte-enseigne* (standard-bearer)
- 1 surgeon
- 1 fourier
- 6 *Rottmeister* or corporals
- 3 fifers

- 3 drummers
- 96 Swiss guards
- 4 carpenters
- 2 archers (*Fourier-Schutzen*) of the captain
- 8 oboists

The monthly cost for the unit was 1,000 Thalers.

Service

For service, the unit could split into six detachments of 30 men under an officer. When smaller detachments were required, 20 men were put under the command of a *Wwachtmeister* and 12 men under a *rottmeister*. For the ordinary service at palace, or *Wachtdienst* (guard-service), a division (*abteilung*) consisting of two detachments was required. This way, every day, an officer, 2 *Rottmeister*, 1 drummer, 1 fifer, 32 Swiss guards, 4 carpenters and 8 oboists were on guard duty. On parade, 2 more drummers were added.

Normally eleven posts were watched by the Swiss in the Palace of Dresden these posts were increased to twelve when the King of Poland added two new rooms to the Residential Castle:

- A post in front of the Green Vault (the Europe's most splendid treasure chamber museum)
- A post in front of the Royal Prince Apartment
- A post near the Royal Princess Apartment at the winding staircase
- A post nearby the Royal Prince bedchamber near the chapel
- A post in the Serene Highness young princes' parade, near the Ballroom
- A post in the Serene Highness young princes' bedchamber near the Brother alley
- A post near the *Schweizer-Hauptmann*
- Two posts at the front gates when closed
- A post at the Middle Tower in the large castle's courtyard
- A post was at the Green Tower.

The Uniform of the Swiss Lifeguards

In 1725, the Swiss Lifeguards received two expensive uniforms, the first for parade and the second for service. The high costs of these uniforms were paid apart. The expense was of 6,000 to 7,000 thalers for the German dress. At every change, also officers had to renew their uniform. They received an indemnity amounting to between 230 and 270 Thalers, for the service uniform and 500–600 thalers for the gala uniform.

The service dress or German dress (*Deutsche-Montur*) consisted of a coat, a waistcoat and breeches of the same cut as the rest of the army. The collarless coat had a lemon yellow field. On the right shoulder, a silver *aiguillette* was hanging. The cuffs, turnbacks, waistcoat and breeches were of sky-blue colour. These were the traditional colours of the House of Wettin. The gaiters were white. The German uniform was to be renewed every three years.

The *Schweitzer* or *Gala-Montur* was changed every six-eight years with an expense of 7,000 to 10,000 thalers. The *Schweitzer* or Gala dress was inspired by the Swiss costume of the sixteenth century. It consisted of a yellow and sky blue baggy coat and trousers with silver lacing. A black cocked hat, silver edged with plumes and sky blue stocks completed the dress.

The unit received special pole arms and swords peculiar to this unit. Examples of NCOs and Swiss halberds are surviving in Berlin.

When the Seven Year War erupted in 1756 the Swiss Lifeguards still retained the two dresses. A plate from the former De Ridder Collection (now in the Bibliothèque Nationale de France) shows a Swiss Guard in German uniform in 1756. A new bandolier was adopted to suspend the peculiar sabre of the unit. The double breasted coat had the large frontal buttons arranged in 1:2:3. Buttonholes were laced in silver. The gaiters were abandoned for silken sky-blue socks and black shoes. The Swiss were still armed with a halberd. The NCOs' halberd was golden with a weaving white metal blade. They had muskets at their disposal in a rack during the Grand Guard, as prescribed. The use of white gloves was mandatory.

The Swiss Lifeguard serving outside the Residence in cold weather wore on the service dress a peculiar garment. A plate from a manuscript in the Deutsches Historisches Museum in Berlin, shows a Swiss Guard wearing the *Mantel* (greatcoat) in 1756.

9

Garde du Corps

The history and origin of the Garde du Corps (also spelt Garde du Korps) are closely linked with the pride and glamour of the ancient lineage of the House of Wettin. The origins of this regiment were claimed to lie as far back as to the ages of the crusaders – more ancient then the annals of the French Maison du Roi – however true, or not. The forming of this Garde could be traced back into very distant ages, initially forming as *Kreuzritter* (crusaders). A well-documented guard unit existed as far back as 1553, under the rule of Duke August I. Under *Hofmarschall* Heinrich von Schoenberg, it consisted of 6 *Kammerjunker* (also called *Kaemmerlige*), 6 *Junker*, 1 captain with 40 armed men on foot, 4 *Rittmeister* (captain) each commanding 15 *Roessern* (horsemen). This unit was terribly expensive. Duke August paid his guard 600 gulden per month for the troops, plus five horses and 400 gulden per year to the commander. The guards accompanied always their master. For example, when August enjoyed hunting, as in September 1584. This memorable hunt lasted ten days and a detailed order of service with the guard's names for each day still remains.

In 1558, August's son Christian I ordered a military parade at Dresden. The full complement of 44 horse-guards, under the *Reiter-Hauptmann* Job von Milckau, paraded that day right under the Residence's windows. The *Hofmarschall* Wolf von Schoenberg zu Pulsnitz, brother of Caspar, at the time Marshal of France, headed the corps.

On 2 January 1590, the Horse guards were formed in four *rotten* (a *rotte* was the equivalent of a squadron). Christian II succeeded his father as Elector of Saxony in 1591 at the age of eight. Because of his youth, his kinsman, Duke Friedrich William I of Saxe-Weimar, assumed the regency of the Electorate until 1601, when Christian was declared an adult and began to govern. He died in Dresden in 1611. Having left no issue, on his death his brother Johann Georg succeeded him as Elector. The geographical position of the Electorate of Saxony, rather than her high standing among the German Protestants, gave her ruler much importance during the Thirty Years War. The Saxon army then consisted of a total of 1,200 horses, 7,000 infantrymen, 1,600 *Reiters*.

In 1620 the horsemen formed a *Hoffahne* (Court-Banner). The standard, made of embroidered silk, had red field with gold and silver motives. On a side the motto UTERQUE TEMPORE PACIS ET BELLI. On reverse the ducal crown over the motto A DEO PRO IMPERIO. On February 1624, the Elector of Brandenburg visited Dresden. The Elector Johann Georg was accompanied by no less than 600 mounted followers. These expensive guards were soon disbanded, on 6 May 1624.

On 1 June 1624, *Hofmarschall* Bernard von Starscheld raised the Leibgarde zu Ross with a strength of 60 horsemen. In 1631, a new unit was raised. It was officially designated as Leibkompagnie Einspänniger. In 1635, the unit was reorganised in two companies (1st and 2nd Leibkompagnie).

In 1644, the unit it was renamed Leibeskadron Einspänniger. In 1648, the unit once more adopted the title of Leibkompagnie Einspänniger. Thereafter in 1671, it consisted of one Kompagnie Einspänniger, one Kompagnie Kroaten (Croats), and one Kompagnie Dragoner being now entitled Deutsche Leibgarde zu Roß. In 1681, the unit became known as the Leibtrabantengarde zu Pferde. In 1686, its name changed again to Gardetrabanten zu Roß. In 1692, it became the Garde du Corps; in 1693, the Leibgardetrabanten zu Roß; in 1699, the Leibgarde zu Pferde; in 1701, the Trabantengarde zu Roß. In October 1701, the unit was reorganized as Garde du Corps, incorporating the former Grandmusketärs,[1] Karabiniers, and Grenadiers zu Pferde. In 1704, the unit was renamed Garde zu Pferde; in 1705, the Garde du Corps; in 1707, the Garde zu Pferde; and finally, from 1710, retained the name of Garde du Corps.

During the 17th century, the Garde du Corps took part in all campaigns of the Saxon army. In 1683, the unit was present at the relief of Vienna, along with Elector Johann Georg III and along with Georg IV on the Rhine. Under August II, it fought in Hungary and Poland.

During the War of the Spanish Succession, in 1704, the Garde du Corps formed in 4 corps: 1st Trabanten, 2nd Karabiniers, 3rd Grenadiers zu Pferde, and 4th Dragoner under the command of General Graf von Flemming and the Generals von Jordan, von Reichenau, and Graf von Tiefenhausen, second in command. Each corps comprised three brigades whose commanders were either ranking generals or Polish grandees. However, a few years later, this organisation was changed in favour of squadrons and companies. In 1756, this regiment consisted of 8 companies in 4 squadrons for a total of some 649 men.

The Chefs of the Regiment:

1697 *General* Graf von Trautmannsdorf
1699 *General* Fürst Lubomirsky
1700 *General-Lieutenant* von Jordan
1701 *General-Lieutenant* Graf von Flemming
1704 *General-Lieutenant* von Jordan

---

1   The *Grandmusketärs* counted 165 men and had been raised in February 1699 by General Graf von Löwenhaupt. Not to be confused with the *Grandmusketärs* at the camp of Zeithain, also counting 165 men in 2 companies, raised in July 1730 by the crown sword-bearer Fürst Lubomirsky. They had been send back to Poland and financed by its treasury until their reduction.

Uniform Plates by Franco Saudelli

1 2

A1: Friedrich August, Graf von Rutowsky;
A2: Friedrich August II.

See Colour Plate Commentaries for further information.

B1: Graf Heinrich von Brühl; B2: Johann Georg von Sachsen (aka Chevalier de Saxe).

See Colour Plate Commentaries for further information.

1

2

3

C1: Swiss Lifeguard wearing the service German uniform; C2: Swiss Lifeguard wearing
the gala Swiss uniform; C3: Swiss Lifeguard wearing *mantel*.

See Colour Plate Commentaries for further information.

1

2

D1: Cadet in service dress; D2: Cadet in gala dress.

See Colour Plate Commentaries for further information.

E1: Officer of the Garde du Corps; E2: *Trabant* (Horseman) of the Garde du Corps.

See Colour Plate Commentaries for further information.

F1: Staff officer of the Regiment Garde du Corps in Gala dress.

See Colour Plate Commentaries for further information.

G1: *General-Lieutenant* Friedrich Heinrich Eugen von Anhalt-Dessau;
G2: Cuirassier Regiment von Vitzthum; G3: Leib-Cuirassier Regiment.

See Colour Plate Commentaries for further information.

H1: Mounted dragoon of Prinz Albrecht Chevauxlegers in service dress.

See Colour Plate Commentaries for further information.

1704 Graf Jacob Heinrich von Flemming

1713 *Generalmajor* Graf von Sapieha

1716 Archduke von Sachsen-Weissenfels

1736 Graf von Rutowsky

1740 Johann Georg, Chevalier de Saxe (resigned in 1763)

1763 Graf von Cosel (died in 1770)

The *Kommandeur* of the regiment was:

1726 *Generalmajor* von Birchholz, then *General-Lieutenant*

1734 *Generalmajor* von Polenz, he died as *General der Kavallerie*

1752 *General-Lieutenant* Graf Vitzthum von Eckstädt, he resigned at the end of the war

1763 *Generalmajor* von Winckelmann, he died in 1776.

Service

During the War of the Polish Succession, in 1733, the Garde du Corps took part in the campaign in Pomerania. From 1733 to 1735, it campaigned in Poland. During the War of the Austrian Succession, in 1741, 1742, 1744 and 1745, the Garde du Corps served in Bohemia and Saxony.

At the end of August 1756, when Friedrich II invaded Saxony, the regiment retired to Pirna with the rest of the Saxon army. At Pirna, the regiment was deployed on the right wing under von Arnim, as part of von Rechenberg's Brigade. The Prussians blockaded the Saxon army in Pirna from September 9 until October 15 when the Saxons finally had to surrender. The Saxon Garde du Corps was then forcibly incorporated into the Prussian Garde du Corps. It is really hard to ascertain how many guards remained in Prussian service. It seems that most of the men absconded. In 1757, the men who had deserted the Prussian service rallied in Hungary. From 1758 to 1761, these men served as foot grenadiers. In 1761, a new horse regiment on 4 squadrons in 8 companies was raised from men of the former Garde du Corps as well as from the other cuirassier regiments. After the Seven Years War, in 1764, only one squadron of the Garde du Corps was retained, the six other squadrons were distributed among the re-raised cuirassiers regiments to serve as carabineer companies.

Garde du Corps. Staff officer.
On mounted service in cold weather, this high rank officer is wearing an ample dark red coat with *bleumourant* collar and large cuffs richly embroidered in gold over an enamelled black cuirass. Under the cuirass, the officer is wearing his buff collarless waistcoat called a *lederkoller*. This thick garment is capable of withstanding the tear and wear of the heavy armour. The waistcoat have *bleumourant* turnbacks edged gold. The gold/crimson interwoven sash around the waist is peculiar of the officer corps. The walking cane with gold fitting was used by all gentlemen. (Original artwork by Franco Saudelli)

Uniforms

The Garde du Corps regiment was a heavy cavalry unit and as an elite unit was issued with particularly expensive and elegant equipment. They had a campaign/service dress called 'interim' dress, an exercise (*exerzier*) dress and finally a gala dress. The cuirass was worn only on campaign.

The principal item was the *Koller* (also spelt *Kollet*). It was a resistant coat, peculiar garment of the heavy cavalry. Once made of elk leather, it was later made of kersey. The coat was of traditional a pale-yellow colour (*paille*). The garment was edged with a light-blue (*bleumourant*) lace made of wool with two yellow stripes through it. Lemon yellow and *bleumourant* were the colours of the court livery of House Wettin. The *Koller* had a small standing collar. The *Koller* had no buttons on the front and was fastened with a series of invisible hooks. Over the *Koller* the trabant could wear the cuirass. A plastron made of iron, padded with tissue and edged in yellow. Leather trousers, high boots, a white belt, leather gloves and cocked hat completed the campaign dress.

The interim dress was characterized by a second coat to wear over the *Koller*. This coat was made of wool and his field colour was a crimson red. The facing colour was *bleumourant* and was on the collar; the cuffs and

M1752 Standard of the Garde du Corps..
The Garde du Corps received in 1730 four identical Standards (*Leibstandarten*). New standards, differing only for minimal details, were issued in 1752. The white silk standards were embroidered with gold and had a gold fringe. Reverse: centre device consisting of a shield carrying the Electoral Saxon arms (left upper canton black, left lower canton white, two red crossed swords superimposed on the left cantons, right side consisting of alternating black and yellow with a green crown-like diagonal band), surmounted by a crimson electoral hat and surrounded by green palm leaves. Obverse: white field heavily embroidered in gold; centre device consisting of the golden royal cipher on a pedestal surmounted by a royal crown and surrounded by green palm leaves. (original artwork by the author)

the turnbacks were in the facing colour. Until 1748, the coat had lapels in the facing colour. The exercise dress comprised a third white coat with *bleumourant* collar, cuffs, and lapels. The armament issued was a couple of pistols in the saddle holsters, a carbine and the straight bladed heavy sabre or *Pallash*. The horse furniture issued was a *bleaumourant* saddlecloth with white edging with two *bleumourant* stripes passed through with white royal monogram for service.

NCOs had a cocked hat with gold edging and officers had also a white feather. Officers had *bleumourant* saddlecloth and pistol holsters with golden lace. NCOs and men had also a second *bleumourant* saddlecloth for parade with yellow edging and the Saxon coat of arms with crown.

A crimson sleeveless supervest also called 'tabard', edged in gold lace, characterized the Gala dress of officers and NCOs. A large emblem on the chest was a gold sun with sky-blue centre. The golden embroidery could have different motives with the royal monogram or the Hebraic name of God. The tabard was worn over a crimson edged gold waistcoat.

Trumpeters and Kettledrummers wore a lemon-yellow coat with *bleumourant* collar, cuffs and lapels. The silver braid had two *bleumourant* velvet stripes through it.

10

Karabiniersgarde

In 1713, the regiment (also spelled Carabiniersgarde) belonged to the reigning Markgrave of Ansbach-Bayreuth. It entered service in the army of King Augustus II as a regiment of dragoons. Until 1717 it served in the campaigns in Poland and Pomerania, and with the reduction of the army in 1717, it incorporated the remainder of the Queen's Cuirassiers. In 1729, the regiment was named Karabiniersgarde and it was augmented with contributions of the other cavalry regiments, much embellished. During the War of the Polish Succession, the regiment served in Poland from 1733 to 1735. During the War of the Austrian Succession, 1740, 1742, 1744, and 1745; the regiment served in Poland, Bohemia, Silesia and Saxony. In 1749, it counted four companies. By 1754, the regiment garrisoned Warsaw. From 1757 to 1763, it fought with the Austrian armies. In 1756, this regiment formed eight companies in four squadrons with 514 men.

The Chef from1748 was *Generalmajor* von Rex (died in 1763 as a *General-Lieutenant*); he was succeeded by *General-Lieutenant* Graf von Brühl who held the post until 1786.

The *Kommandeur* in 1748 was Wolf Kaspar von Zezschwitz (died in 1761); he was succeeded by *Generalmajor* von Wikedé who was in turn succeeded in 1763 by *Oberst* Graf von Callenberg (died in 1767).

In 1764, the regiment was renamed Karabiniersgarde.

Uniform
The unit's uniform was very close to the uniform issued to the Regiment *Garde du Corps*. The headwear was the black cocked hat with gold trim and white rosette on the left side.

The coats in 1730–33 were white with lapels in the red facing colour. The coat lost the lapels in 1735. The troopers had a red waistcoat but in 1735, the field color changed to pale (straw) yellow. The officers wore a red waistcoat until 1738, like in the infantry at that time. The collarless leather *koller* was buff with horizontal pockets with three brass buttons and was fastened on the front with hooks instead of buttons. The black enameled cuirass was an iron plastron edged in red. The carabiniers wore the cuirasses over the *lederkoller* and in cold weather under the coat. The leather breeches and the high black boots were the same as for the heavy cavalry. The NCO's cuffs were edged in golden lace.

Musician uniform cut varied little during the period. In 1738–44, the coat was yellow with light blue facing on collar, cuffs and turnbacks. The *koller* was *paille* with turnbacks edged red-black-yellow-red-yellow-black-red. The waistcoat was light blue. In 1745–61, the coat was white with scarlet collar, cuffs, and turnbacks. The waistcoat was scarlet with golden lacing but the *Koller* was frequently worn instead. On campaign, the cloak was scarlet with white collar.

The horse furniture consisted of a red saddlecloth edged yellow in which two red stripes, the royal ciphers and crown in yellow. The edges of officers' saddlecloths were in golden lace, as were the ciphers and crown. The trumpeter and kettle-drummer had red coats with white collar, cuffs and turnbacks. The gold lace had two red velvet stripes through it. On each side of the coat's front there were six laces (yellow with two red stripes) arranged 1:2:3. The regiment had silver trumpets for parade, brass trumpets for service. The regiment carried silver kettledrums that were captured from Prussian Dragoon Regiment von Roedll or Holstein on 13 December 1745. Drum banners were possibly red with golden embroideries.

11

Cuirassier Regiments

The Saxon heavy cavalry traditionally comprised the regiments of cuirassiers and dragoons: although the latter retained aspects of the original mounted-infantry service, they were employed in a similar manner to the cuirassiers. In 1730, the army had only four cuirassier regiments: CR1 Kronprinz, CR2 Prinz Friedrich, CR3 von Polenz, and CR4 von Kriegern. Four more regiments were added between 1731 and 1733: CR5 Promnitz/O'Byrn, CR6 Nassau/Minckwitz, CR7 Brand/Minckwitz/l'Annonciade, and CR 8 Gersdorff/Dallwitz, the last-named being converted from the Grenadiers a Cheval in 1733. These regiments fought during the War of Polish Succession, the First and Second Silesian Wars.

The heavy cavalry underwent a major reorganization in 1748 when all but three of the cuirassier regiments and all the dragoon regiments were disbanded and three new cuirassiers regiments were raised. More precisely, five cuirassiers regiment were disbanded (CR4 von Ronnow, CR5 v O'Byrn, CR6 von Minckwitz, CR7 l'Annonciade, and CR8 von Dallwitz). DR1 von Rechenberg, DR3 von Arnim and DR4 von Plötz were converted into cuirassier regiments. As far DR 2 was concerned, personnel were melded with CR4 von Vitzthum. Six cuirassier regiments were therefore in service between 1748 and 1756.

From 1733, the strength of a cuirassier regiment was 351 men on two squadrons each of two 85-man companies, and an 11-man staff. During the Silesian Wars, each regiment was on paper composed of three squadrons of two 95-man companies giving a total of 621 horsemen. In reality, only in October 1745 did the cuirassiers parade in three squadrons in the front of the Elector. On campaign the strength was always eroded and only two squadrons could be fielded. The Saxon cavalry formed up in two or three ranks. The use or firearms was practiced but instructions called for charging at a gallop relaying on 'cold steel' only. Each regiment had a train of 33 wagons and 150 horses.

The peacetime establishment, according to the 1753 Regulations, was on four squadrons for a total of 514 men and 394 horses. The Saxon army paraded in 1753 at Uebingau and Rutowsky observed how a Saxon army so reduced could not defend his country. Every complaint was futile and the Prime Minister Graf von Brühl simply ignored him. The monarch lived isolated, or surrounded by personal controlled by the ever-present Minister, and almost any attempt to talk with the Elector was frustrated by the rigid rules dictated by Brühl himself in 1755.

All six Cuirassier Regiments and the Garde du Corps capitulated at Pirna, in October 1756. The personnel were incorporated in the Prussian army but except for the Garde du Corps the horsemen deserted in mass. The German term 'Revertenten' (a neologism, also spelt *Reverdenten*, derived from the Latin verb Revertere, indicating someone who is coming back) was used since then instead of the negative term deserters, referring to these men who valiantly served in Austrian service or in French pay for the rest of the war. The men served on foot in grenadier companies until 1761, when a new cavalry regiment was formed.

Uniforms

The cuirassier uniform was very like that worn by several armies of the age. Prussian and Austrian cuirassiers wore a very similar uniform. It changed only slightly during the whole period. The distinctive element of was the cuirass, which was worn only in combat. The single front-plate was just an iron plastron modelled to fit the thorax of the horsemen, to whom it was secured by leather straps running along the front of the waist of the cuirass and crossing over the wearer's back. Cuirasses were enameled black on the front to prevent rust, with edges embellished by edges in the facing colour. The interior side was padded to reduce friction on the coat. The officers' cuirass was richly decorated by means of metal fittings in gold or silver around the neck and the end of the slings. In the middle of the cuirass front there was the royal monogram surmounted by a crown. Under the cuirass a coatee was worn. In the 1730s these garments were still made of natural leather or 'buffalo' of a shade that could change with use from a white yellow to a light brown. Subsequently, this coatee, called in German 'Kollet' (also spelt *Koller*), presumably due to the shortage of elk's leather was made of a white woolen kersey. Warmer and more breathable even if less expensive to manufacture, the kersey Kollet maintained, thanks to his thickness, defensive properties like the leather. The garments were never washed. Spots and discolouration were covered over by regular chalking, similar to the pipeclay treatment used in England.

The design of the coat was oriented toward the older leather version. The *kollet* had short skirts with wide turnbacks, cuffs, and folding collar in the facing colour; the front edge ran almost straight to under the waist, with a light curve under the breast, in order to obtain the necessary width for the wearer. The edges met in the middle of the breast and had neither lapels nor buttons and were closed with invisible but robust hooks and eyes at intervals of 3.5 to 4 cm. A wide strip of regimental lace edged both side of the breast opening (not quite up to neck) and continued around the edge of the turnbacks; similar lace edged the top and rear opening of the cuffs. On the left shoulder, there was a white shoulder strap piped in the facing colour to secure the straps of the cuirass.

This coat was normally reserved for parade in cold weather and not for field service. Over the cuirass the heavy horsemen could wear a second coat. This coat was also white, since 23 July 1734 when the field colour was changed from dark red. This loose garment was left open on the front. Two rows of eight ornamental large buttons arranged in four pairs were on the front. They were useless. The coat had wide cuffs, falling collar and turnbacks in the facing colour. On the side the coat had two pockets with leaflets closed by three small metal buttons. Two buttons were sewed on the back at the waist. Beneath the *Kollet*, was worn a waistcoat of the facing colour edged down the front and around the skirts of a narrower lace in the regimental pattern.

Table 1 The Cuirassiers Regiments Facing Colours 1734–1748

	Kollet	Collar, waistcoat, cuffs & turnbacks	Buttons
CR1 ('*Leib-regiment*')	Light buff (*Paille*)	Sky blue (*Bleumourant*)	Yellow metal
CR2	Light buff (*Paille*)	Sky blue (*Bleumourant*)	White metal
CR3	Light buff (*Paille*)	Light blue (until 1737) then dark blue (*Dunkelblau*)	Yellow metal
CR4	Light buff (*Paille*)	Lemon yellow (*Zitrongelb*)	White metal
CR5	Light buff (*Paille*)	Yellow (*Gelb*)	Yellow metal
CR6	Light buff (*Paille*)	Red (*Rot*)	Yellow metal
CR7	Light buff (*Paille*)	Green (*Grun*)	White metal
CR8	1734–1746 Light red (*Hellrot*) then *Paille*	Light red (*Hellrot*) then White (1744)	White metal

Table 2 The Cuirassiers Regiments Facing Colours 1748–1756

	Collar, waistcoat, cuffs & turnbacks	Buttons
CR1	Red (*Rot*)	Yellow metal
CR2	Sky blue (*Bleumourant*)	White metal
CR3	Dark blue (*Dunkelblau*)	Yellow metal
CR4	Yellow (*Gelb*)	White metal
CR5	Green (*Grun*)	White metal
CR6	Orange (*Orange*)	White metal

Breeches and gauntlets were white and long white stockings were worn under the high black riding boots. On the knee a protection against continuous rubbing was worn, called in French, the '*manchette*'. The regular headwear was the cocked hat. Per the 1753 Regulation, the front horn should be exactly positioned at the external limit of the left eyebrow. The hat was made of a thick black felt and was embellished by coloured cords and rosettes in the side corners. At the left front, there was a white fabric or paper cockade secured by a black loop with a button at the lower end. The officers' hat was edged by a metal lace (golden or silver according to the regimental facing).

The sabre, like in Prussia called '*Pallash*', was suspended from a waist belt of leather painted in white (until 1735 it was left in natural colour) with brass fittings.

Regimental Details

In the list, which follow the regimental Chefs are given. Each regiment was customarily only referred to by the name of the proprietary colonel or *Chef*, usually a general officer. The traditional system caused a certain amount of confusion related to the sometime repeating family name, by the relatively frequent changing of the proprietor. The anciently of service of the proprietor, also conditioned the priority in the series of a regiment or another. Traditions were strong in the army and only after 1755 were units allocated a number to indicate seniority. The attribution of numbers to units in existence prior to that date is adopted for clarity, the system being that given in *Verzeichnis alter selbststaendigen Truppentheile der ehemals kurfuerstlich, jetzt koeniglich saechsischen Armee.*

CR1 Leib-Cuirassier Regiment (1680–1806)

Raised as a cavalry regiment in 1680, it become a cuirassiers regiment in 1697. Capitulated in 1756. A new regiment was formed in 1763.

Chef:

1697 Graf Trautmannsdorff

1699 La Forest

1700 Kurprinz

1713 Königlicher Prinz

1726 Kronprinz

1733 Leib-Regiment

1756 Disbanded and newly raised in 1763.

During the War of the Polish Succession, in 1734, the regiment campaigned in Poland. The same year, it was officially entitled '*Leibregiment*'. In 1735, it served on the Rhine. During the War of the Austrian Succession, in 1741, 1742, 1744 and 1745, the regiment served with the Saxon army in Bohemia and Saxony.

CR2 Königlicher Prinz (Royal Prince)

Chef:

1703 von Flemming

1706 Prinz Alexander

1727 Prinz Friedrich

1733 Kurprinz

1734–1756 Königlicher Prinz Friedrich Christian

1756 Disbanded and newly raised in 1763.

CR3 Maffei/Vitzthum (1702–1778)

Chef:

1702 von Tiesenhausen

1704 von Gersdorff

1706 aus dem Winckel

1713 Althann

1714 von Kyau

1715 von Arnstaedt

1717 von Pflugk

1728 von Hackeborn

1730 von Polenz

1734 Venediger

1738 Maffei

1745 von Vitzthum

1756 Disbanded and newly raised in 1763.

CR4 Haudring/Ronnow (1694–1748)

Chef:

1694 von Bunau

1698 Lubomirsky

1699 von Stainau

1706 von Damnitz

1713 Johnston

1715 von Zuhlen

1717 von Kriegern

1735 von Arnim

1740 von Haudring

1746 von Ronnow

1748 Disbanded.

CR5 Promnitz/O'Byrn (1732–48)

Chef:

1732 Promnitz

1741 Johann Jacob O'Byrn

1748 Disbanded

CR6 Nassau/Minckwitz (1731–48)

Chef:

1731 von Nassau

1745 Minckwitz

1748 Disbanded

CR7 Brand/Minckwitz/L'Annonciade (1732–1748)

Chef:

1732 von Brand

1735 Minckwitz

1745 von Bestenwbostel

1746 L'Annonciade

1748 Disbanded

CR8 Gersdorff/Dallwitz (1730–1748)

Formed in 1730 as Grenadier a Cheval Regiment with four companies and the next year renamed Prinz Christian Dragoons. In 1732 received two more companies and in 1733 formed the CR8 Saxen-Gotha.

Chef:

1730 Sachsen-Gotha

1731 Prinz Christian Sachsen-Gotha

1733 Sachsen-Gotha

1741 Gersdorff

1745 Johann Friedrich von Dallwitz (alslo spelt Dallwig)

1748 Disbanded.

The three new regiments raised in 1748:

CR4 Rechenberg/von Anhalt-Dessau (1748–1806)

Chef:

1748 Rechenberg

1748 Sonderhausen

1749–1756 Eugen von Anhalt-Dessau

1756 Disbanded and newly raised in 1763.

CR5 Plotz (1748–1778)

Chef:

1748 von Plötz

1756 Disbanded

1764 Benkendorff

CR6 von Arnim (also spelt Arnimb)

Chef:

1748–1756 von Arnim

1756 Disbanded and newly raised in 1763

12

Dragoon Regiments

In 1730, the Saxon army had four dragoon regiments. Each regiment had three squadrons of two companies each, plus a grenadier company, consisting of three officers and 2 drummers plus a detachment of one corporal and 10 dragoons. In 1732, the picked men of the grenadier companies of the four regiments were converged to form CR4 von Brand. Every regiment had six 75-man companies formed into three, later two, squadrons with a total of 469 men.

The Dragoon regiments were all disbanded in 1748 and the personnel were merged in the Cuirassiers regiments.

Uniform

The too-expensive dark red field of the dragoon coat was changed in white in 1734, as for the rest of the army except for the guards units. The single-breasted coat had, at first, no lapels but six large buttons on the right side arranged 2:2:2. On the left side was the same number of buttonholes. The DR3 had 9 buttons arranged in 3:3:3. Note that staff officers had coat buttons equally spaced. The coat's collar, cuffs and turnbacks were in the regimental distinctive color. Under the coat troopers wore a light buff waistcoat. Officers' waistcoats were in facing colour. Breeches were in light buff color. On 18 April 1741, dragoon coats received lapels in the facing colour.

Table 3 Dragoon Regiment Facing Colours 1735–1748

Regiment	Coat	Facings	Buttons	Saddlecloth
DR1	White	Yellow	White metal	Red with plain white border lines
DR2	White	Light green	White metal	Red
DR3	White	Sky blue	White metal	Red
DR4	White	Light red	White metal	Scarlet with plain white border lines

Regimental Details

DR1 von Rechenberg

Chef:

1698 Wolfenbuttel

1701 Milckau

1717 von Bircholz

1726 von Arnstaedt I

1732 von Arnstaedt II

1741 von Rechenberg

1748 Became CR4 Rechenberg

DR2 von Schwarzburg-Sondershausen

Chef:

1700 von Goltz

1712 von Flemming

1715 von Bielke

1719 von Diemar

1719 von Sitzen

1724 von Weissenbach

1724 von Katte

1733 von Leipziger

1742 von Schwarzburg-Sondershausen

1748 Disbanded

DR3 von Schlichting

Chef:

1703 Oertzen

1705 Dunewald

1711 Sachsen-Weissenfels

1717 Unruh

1728 Goldhacker

1734 von Schlichtling

1745 von Arnim

1748 Became CR6 von Arnim

DR4 von Plötz

Chef:

1704 Wrangel

1710 Baudissin

1717 Klingenberg

1729 Johann Georg, Chevalier de Saxe

1741 von Pirch

1744 von Plötz

1748 Became CR5 von Plötz

13

Chevauxlegers Regiments

The first cavalry unit of this specialty, also spelt chevaulegers, was raised in Poland in 1733 to provide western-style cavalry using a cheaper breed of small Polish horses that previously had been considered 'unmilitary'. These horses were mostly coppery-red chestnut (sorrels) in lighter shades with the manes and tails in the same colour. A total of four regiments were raised. CLR Prinz Karl, from 1758 Herzog von Kurland, and CLR Graf Brühl, were raised in 1733; CLR Graf Rutowsky was raised in 1742; and finally CLR Prinz Albrecht was raised in 1745. According to the 1753 *État*, each regiment counted 4 squadrons with a nominal strength of some 762 men. The trooper of any of these units was entitled 'dragoon'. CLR Rutowsky was organized in the same manner as a cuirassier regiment and was also in literature commonly referred as a light dragoon regiment. The sole difference between Rutowsky and the other units was their different mounts. CLR Rutowsky was mounted with the German expensive breeds, whereas the others had the cheaper Polish horses.

CLR Graf Rutowsky (Light Dragoons)
The regiment was raised in 1742, in Saxony by *Oberst* Vitzthum von Eckstädt. During the War of the Austrian Succession, the regiment served in the campaigns of 1744 and 1745 in Saxony. At the outbreak of the Seven Years War, in 1756, the regiment consisted of four squadrons, each of two companies, for a total theoretical strength of some 514 men. During the Seven Years War, the regiment had the following *Chefs*: in 1756: *Feldmarschall* Graf von Rutowsky; from 1762: Baron von Sacken, *Oberst* and later *Generalmajor* (died in 1789).

During the Seven Years War, the regiment had the following commanders: since 1745: *Oberst* Baron von Dyherrn, later *General-Lieutenant* (died in 1759 from the wounds suffered at the Battle of Bergen), from 1759: *Oberst* von Schlieben (promoted *Generalmajor* in 1761 becoming commander, during the war, of the unique newly raised heavy cavalry regiment, and killed in 1762 in the second combat of Lutterberg).

In 1763, the regiment reformed in 4 squadrons by incorporating the Frei-Husaren von Schill squadron. The latter received 'German' dragoon uniforms in 1764.

At the end of August 1756, when Friedrich II proceeded to the invasion of Saxony, the regiment retired to Pirna with the rest of the Saxon army. At Pirna, the regiment was deployed on the right wing under von Arnim, as part of Rechenberg's Brigade. The Prussians blockaded the Saxon army in Pirna from 9 September until 15 October when the Saxons finally had to surrender. The regiment was then incorporated into the Prussian Herzog von Württemberg Dragoons. In 1757, two bodies, under Sergeants Ehring and Heysing, and a third, under Corporal Eichler, escaped Prussian service and reached Moravia where they were distributed among the other Chevauxlegers regiments. Both sergeants were made captains, and Corporal Eichler was promoted cornet in 1761. The remaining dragoons served as grenadiers with the Saxon infantry till 1761. That year, they were re-mounted for cavalry service.

The regiment's uniform included a peculiar dark red coat. The lapels, collar, cuffs and turnbacks were of the black facing colour. The waistcoat was straw. The breeches were straw or white. The eight buttons in golden metal were arranged on the lapels in 2: 2: 2: 2. The undercoat was buff from 1745 until 1753.

CLR Prinz Karl, 1758 Herzog von Kurland

The regiment was raised in 1733. It originally consisted of two squadrons of mounted *Jägers* serving in Poland. In 1735, it was augmented to four squadrons entitled Prinz Karl Chevaulegersregiment. During the War of the Polish Succession, the regiment took part in the campaigns of 1734 and 1735 in Poland. During the War of the Austrian Succession, the regiment took part in the campaigns of 1742. In 1743, it was stationed in Lithuania. In 1744, it was posted along the border in Upper Lusatia. In 1745, the regiment was initially at the great camp of Rückmersdorf near Leipzig. In November, when the Prussians occupied Saxony, an Austro-Saxon army marched to Wilsdruff. On December 15, this army was defeated by the Prussians at the Battle at Kesselsdorf. The regiment then went to Kaden (present day Kadaň, Czech Republic) and Postelberg (present day Postoloprty, Czech Republic). From 1746, the regiment garrisoned Sambor in Poland. In 1752, the regiment went to Grodno during the Imperial Diet before returning to Sambor. By 1754, the regiment was still garrisoning Sambor. At the outbreak of the Seven Years War, in 1756, the regiment consisted of eight companies in four squadrons for a book strength of some 762 men. Its service during the Seven Years War is detailed in Chapter 5.

During the Seven Years War, the *Chef* of the regiment was: until 1758: Prinz Karl von Sachsen, from 1758: Prinz Karl von Sachsen, Duke of Kurland (the same *Chef*, who was now Duke of Kurland). The commander of the regiment was: from 1756 to December 1757: *Oberst-Lieutenant* Prittwitz, from December 1757 to 1765: *Oberst* von Benkendorff.

CLR Prinz Karl received in 1733 a mix of uniforms related to its origins. The first and second companies were uniformed as dragoons with a red coat with deep blue facings and brass buttons. The third and fourth companies, raised from *jägers*, received a dark green coat with yellow facings and brass buttons. The coat had no lapels. In 1734, the coat was red for all

four companies. In 1738, the coat field changed to parrot green with red as a facing colour on the collar, the cuffs and the turnbacks. The front had no lapels and the brass buttons were arranged in pairs 1:2:3. The breeches were straw or white. The saddlecloth was parrot green with yellow border, cipher and crown.

The *Leibfahne* was a white silk square embroidered with a central gold ornate device, in rococo fashion, carrying a quartered shield with the arms of Poland and Lithuania (eagle & knight) in white. A golden/scarlet royal crown surmounted the shield laying on a pale green palm leaves. The four corners carried the gold royal monogram "AR". The standard had gold fringe. The final was gold.

CLR Prinz Albrecht

The regiment was raised in 1745 in the Marienburg area (the Teutonic Order's Castle of Marienburg in Poland) by *Oberst* von Wilmsdorf and soon later employed along the Silesian border.

Each Chevauleger Regiment carried four standards: a Colonel's Standard (*Leibfahne*) and three Regimental Standards (*Ordinarfahne*). The first Colonel's Standard was issued to CL1 Prinz Karl, on 6 May 1735. The other regiments received identical Colonel's Standards respectively: CL2 on 1748, CL3 on 1747 and CL4 on May 1743.

The three Regimental Standards had a field in the facing colour (CL1 red, CL2 sky blue, CL3 crimson, and CL4 red) with a centre device consisting of the gold monogram of the King of Poland "AR3" surmounted by a royal crown. The standard was gold fringed. (Original artwork by the author)

By 1754, the regiment garrisoned Biezun. At the outbreak of the Seven Years War, in 1756, the regiment consisted of four squadrons, each of two companies, for a theoretical total of some 762 men. Throughout the Seven Years War, the Chef of the regiment was *General-Lieutenant* Prinz Albrecht of Saxony and Poland, Duke of Sachsen-Teschen. During the Seven Years War, the effective commander of the regiment was since 1754 *Generalmajor* von Monro and from 1759 to 1764 *General-Lieutenant* Graf von Renard (who received his own regiment in 1764).

In 1756, during the invasion of Saxony by the Prussians, the regiment was stationed around Kraków in Poland. By 11 October, it counted 544 men and 510 horses. Being stationed in Poland, it avoided the fate of the Saxon units captured at Pirna who were forcefully incorporated into the Prussian service. Its subsequent service during the Seven Years War is detailed in Chapter 5.

When raised, CLR Prinz Albrecht received a green-gray coat with black as a facing colour. Collar, lapels, cuffs, and turnbacks were made of black velvet. On the lapels two rows of eight white metal buttons were arranged in pairs 2:2:2:2. Two more buttons were allocated under the lapels. Saddle cover and holster covers were red. Officers' holster covers were yellow lined in golden metal sporting a crowned royal monogram. The pairs of buttons, now in golden metal (brass for troopers) on the lapels were reduced to three.

CLR Graf Brühl

The regiment was raised in 1733 under its commander *Oberst* Sibilski and immediately sent to Poland. It consisted of two squadrons formed with troopers contributed by various regiment of the Saxon Army.

During the War of the Polish Succession, in 1733, the regiment served in Poland along with *Oberst* Vitzthum von Eckstädt's Mounted *Jägers*, where they engaged in numerous 'coups', especially threatening Greater Poland during the siege of Danzig. In 1735, the regiment was increased to four squadrons and designated as Chevauxlegers.

At the beginning of the War of the Austrian Succession, the regiment consisted of eight companies. It took part in the campaigns of 1742, 1744 and 1745. On 13 December 1745, along with some *Uhlans*, it charged the Prussian rearguard near Lommatsch and Zehren, capturing three standards and two pairs of silver kettle drums. By 1754, the regiment garrisoned Warsaw. In 1756, during the invasion of Saxony by the Prussians, the regiment was stationed around Kraków in Poland. By October 11, it counted 757 men and 725 horses. Being stationed in Poland, it avoided the fate of the Saxon units captured at Pirna who were forcefully incorporated into the Prussian service. Its service during the Seven Years War is detailed in Chapter 5.

In 1756 the regiment consisted of 8 companies formed in 4 squadrons for a total book strength of some 762 men. The successive chefs of the regiment were: from 1733, *Oberst* Sibilski, Baron von Wolfsberg; from 1748, General Graf von Brühl (died in 1763); from 1763, *Oberst* Hans Moritz Graf von Brühl; from 1764, *General-Lieutenant* Graf von Renard (resigned in 1778). During the Seven Years War, the commander of the regiment was since 1753: *Oberst* von Gößnitz (died as a *General-Lieutenant* in 1763), from 1763: *Oberst* von Diepow (died in 1771).

When raised by von Sybilsky, the regiment received a green-greyish coat with *bleumourant* as a facing colour on collar, lapels and turnbacks. On the lapels there were eight buttons arranged in pairs 2:2:2:2: with two more button and loops on the front after the lapel. The horse equipment and the pistol-holster covers had a red field. This uniform was modified in 1748 when the Prime Minister von Brühl succeeded Sybilsky as a *Chef* of the unit. The now six buttons on the lapels were arranged in three pairs. The previously *bleumourant* undercoat was changed to a buff colour. This garment was retained until 1753. The dragoons of CLR Graf Brühl initially had a peculiar cap, high fronted and made of felt covered by sky blue cloth. The high front was embroidered with the royal cipher and crown and was piped in white lace with a thin scarlet line. This cap appears in a plate by Trache and in the monumental work of Richard Knötel. The manuscript of the DHM in Berlin, dated 1756, shows that this cap was no more in use. The standard cocked hat, common to all the four regiments, was used instead until the end of the Seven Years War.

14

Polish Uhlan *Pulks* – *Uhlanen* or Tatars

The Polish horsemen recruited in Lithuania and from Tatars were referred in German as *Uhlanen*. The uhlan units were raised and maintained by the Polish Commonwealth and during the 18th century hired into Saxon service. When into Saxon service they were considered 'irregular troops' because their companies called *Fahnen* or *Hof-Fahnen* (literally banneret or flags) were not 'standing' units but could be hired or disbanded at will. A variable number of *Fahnen*, usually from six to eight, were grouped into a *pulk* (in Polish a regiment).

The uhlans had a long tradition of service into Polish Commonwealth. Although also armed with a lance they were a light mounted infantry and each company had a drummer like the French dragoons. They could fight both on horse or on foot. In 1730, at the military summer camp at Zeithain, two *Fahnen*, distinguished by blue and red facing, were already in Saxon service. The companies maintained the internal and external security of the tent village and acted as escort of the intervening noble personalities. They participated in all campaigns from 1735 onwards. During peacetime, they secured the roads between Dresden and Warsaw.

During the War of Polish Succession, the uhlans remained loyal to the House of Wettin in contrast to the most of Polish-Lithuanian army which supported Leszczyński. After the end of hostilities in 1735 more *Fahnen* were raised. In 1740, *Oberst* von Bledowsky (also spelt Blentowsky and Belwedowsky) commanded a *pulk* of twelve *Fahnen*. In time of war, more companies were hired on 1 January (13th) 1741 and on 1 May (14th and 15th) of the same year. During the First Silesian War the Uhlan *pulks* acted as scouts, vanguard and rear-guard. Riding their sturdy small Polish horses they could cover in a day long distances. The Austrian hussars were no match for them. As the Austrian light cavalry was unprepared to fight against lancers. In 1741, their fierce appearance and extraordinary endurance attracted the curiosity of the French soldiers, as told in the Chapter 3. They shaved their head and their faces but sported thin long moustaches. This conferred them an evil-aspect that caused fear and respect.

During the winter campaign of 1744 three Uhlan *pulks* (Wilczewsky, Bledowsky and Sychodzinsky) harassed the Prussian columns retiring from Prague, killing with no mercy the isolated parties, making prisoners and collecting deserters.

In December 1745, the irregular cavalry companies were under the command of von Sybilsky was divided in four *pulks* commanded by Bledowsky, Rudnicki, Bertuzewsky, and a new regiment raised only in February 1745. All were present at the crucial battle of Kesselsdorf. In 1748, for economy reasons three *pulks* were disbanded.

Only two *pulks* were kept on Warsaw's provisions budget in March 1757. Each *pulk* had 6 *Hof-Fahnen* (court-banners), 1 banner counting 75 men.

A third *pulk*, the Yellow, under Bertuzewsky, was later re-activated but remained in Poland.

Blue Uhlan *Pulk* Graf Rudnicki

The *pulk* was created early in 1745 from a unit of Tatar Guards of the Principality of Kiev. During the 1740s, a company counted a total of 71 horsemen; 3 officers, 34 *towarczys* (nobles) and 34 *pocztowi* (privates). Composition changed in 1741 when the personnel was increased to a total of 100 men; one *Rittmeister*, one lieutenant, one cornet accompanying the *pocztowi*, one kettle-drummer accompanying the *pocztowi*, 46 *towarczys*, 46 *pocztowi*. In May 17 1745, the unit counted eight *Hof-Fahnen* when it entered Silesia with the Austro-Saxon Army. On December 15, it was present at the Battle of Kesselsdorf, under the command of von Sybilsky. In 1746, after the Treaty of Dresden (December 25 1745), the unit returned to Poland. By 1754, the regiment garrisoned various places in Poland. By 1757, the unit counted 602 men and 575 horses. During the Seven Years War, the regiment was commanded by, since 1733, Sychodzinsky, Czymbaj Murza Rudnicki; from 1762: Bielack (later major general in the Polish Army). In 1764, the unit was transferred to the Polish Army and named 4th *Pulk* Przedniej Straży (4th Regiment of the Forward Guard).

Red Uhlan *Pulk* Graf Renard

The unit was created in late 1744. On December 15, it was present at the Battle of Kesselsdorf, together with the Belwedowsky, Rudnicki, and Bertuzewsky *Pulks* under the command of von Sybilsky. In 1746, after the Treaty of Dresden (December 25 1745), the unit returned to Poland. By 1757, the unit counted 603 men and 575 horses. During the Seven Years' War, the regiment was commanded by, since 1750: Broninowsky; from 1757, Andreas

Uhlan or irregular light cavalryman in 1756 according to the manuscript of the DHM in Berlin. The white calf-length collarless caftan coat is the uniform of the unit. The coat had gold edged loopholes. The regiments or *pulks* fighting during the SYW had distinctive facing colours, blue or red. The wide trousers like the Cossack *Sharavas* are in the facing colours. (Original artwork by Franco Saudelli)

Graf von Renard, and from 1759, Schiebel. In 1764, the unit was transferred to the Polish Army and renamed 5th *Pulk* Przedniej Straży (5th *Pulk* of the Forward Guard).

Yellow Uhlan *Pulk* Graf Bertuzewsky

A third unit was raised in 1745. During the Seven Years War this unit was posted on garrison duty in Poland. A fourth unit was also raised in 1745, of which little is known and which was shortly afterwards disbanded.

Uhlan Uniform 1741–1763

The uhlan uniform was first regulated in 1741 but the dress had changed little since the 17th century. The headwear was a conical cap, with a flattened top and crowned by fur. The coat was a Polish traditional light grey (undyed wool) or white calf-length caftan with low upstanding collar in the regiment facing colour. The inner coat was lined in the facing colour (blue, red, yellow, and green). The coat could be fastened up to show the coloured inside. The cuffs were in the facing colour and could vary in shape from square to pointed. The cuffs-flaps could be present or not, like buttons. A rare manuscript in the collections of the Deutsches Historisches Museum, datable to 1756, shows that the front of the coat was fastened up to the waist by small rounded buttons and was enriched by yellow or white lace (probably metallic for officers) or cordons resembling the hussars.

The trousers were the Polish traditional baggy garment like the Cossack *Sharavas* in the facing colour on parade or in any dark shade on campaign. The equipment consisting in a waist-belt in natural leather and a cross-belt with a suspended cartridge box.

Each non-noble (servant) horseman was issued a pistol and a cartridge box and every *towarczy* (Polish noble) received a carbine. Each horseman had their own sabre and lance. The quality of the steel curved blades was high and any sabre could be personalised with gems and stones. The curved blade was protected by a black or dark scabbard with brass fittings. The lance pennant could show different design but normally were white and facing colour.

Officers had black middle high fur cap. White over-cloth with very wide and long sleeves, a little, low red upstanding collar, red turnbacks and red lining. On the collar, red-white laces and the same lace on the breast where was on the right side (of the middle) four pairs of gilded buttons. On the turnbacks, which reached halfway down the thighs, were in the same red-white lace the crowned AR. Red waistcoat with red-white lacing along edges. Red baggy trousers reaching to the ankles. White-red sash. Black boots without spurs. All bearded, but no pigtails. Red end-pointed saddlecloth with wide gilded border.

Appendix I

Saxon Army Staff 1733

Feldmarschall, Supreme '*Land und Hauszeug*', Master and Governor of Dresden:

1. August Christoph, Graf von Wackerbarth.

Generals:
2. Joachim Friedrich, Graf von Flemming, *General der Kavallerie* and Governor of Lipsia.
3. Wolff Heinrich von Baudissin (sometime written von Baudis), *General der Kavallerie.*
4. Anton, Graf von Luxelburg, *General de Cavalerie.*
5. Johann Adolph, Archduke of Sachsen-Weissenfels, *General der Kavallerie* and *der Infanterie.*
6. Moritz Friedrich von Milckau, *General de Cavalerie.*
7. Adam Heinrich von Bose, *General der Infanterie* and Governor of Wittenberg

General-Lieutenant:
*   Claudius Petrus von St. Paul
*   Joseph, Graf von Sapieha
*   Joh. Adam von Senfertitz
*   Karl Friedrich Gottlob, Graf von Castell, Vice-Governor of Dresden
*   Claude de Brosses
*   Alexander Joseph, Graf von Montmorancy (sic)
*   Johann von Bodt, Chief Ingenieur
*   Moritz von Kavenagk (sic)
*   Friedrich von Zuhlen
*   Georg Ignaz, Fürst Lubomirsky
*   Nic. Faustin, Prince Radzwill
*   Georg Friedrich von Gfug
*   Johann Adam von Diemar

Generalmajor:

1. Caspar Otto von Glasenapp
2. Johann Gottfried Schmidt (artillery)
3. Franz Karl Obmaus (artillery)
4. Rudolph Heinrich von Neitschuss
5. Damm Siegmund von Pflug
6. Alexander von Stotterheim
7. Petrus la Mar
8. Christian August, Baron von Friesen
9. Matthias von Berner
10. Georg Wilhelm von Bircholtz
11. Friedrich August, Graf von Rutowsky
12. Wichmann von Klingenberg
13. Gustav Fissner, commander of Old Dresden
14. Karl Isaac de la Haye
15. Johann Christoph Dresky
16. Jacob Alexander Fürst Lubomirsky
17. Wolff Adolph von Gersdorff
18. Hermann, Baron von Riedesel, commander of Königstein
19. Wolfgang Georg von Marchen, commander of Pleissenburg
20. Woldemar, Baron von Loewendahl
21. Georg Hubert, Baron von Diesbach, captain of the *Trabanten*

Appendix II

Saxon Army Staff 1740

Feldmarschall
> Herzog von Sachsen-Weissenfels Knight of the White Eagle and St. Heinrich order (b. 4/9/1685, d. 16/5/1746).

Generals
> *General der Kavallerie* Joachim Friedrich, Graf von Flemming Governor of Lipsia (b.27/8/1665, d.12/10/1740)
>
> *General der Kavallerie* Wolff Heinrich von Baudis sic. (von Baudissin) Cabinet Minister; Knight of the White Eagle, of St. Heinrich and of Dannebrog Orders (b.1/9/1671, d.24/7/1748).
>
> *General der Kavallerie* Moritz Friedrich von Milckau, Knight of the St. Heinrich Order.
>
> *General der Infanterie* Adam Heinrich von Bose Governor of Wittenberg, Knight of the St. Heinrich Order (b. 3/3/1667, d. 21/5/1749).
>
> *General der Infanterie* Heinrich Friedrich Graf von Friesen, Cabinet Minister and Governor of Dresden, Knight of the White Eagle and of the St. Heinrich Order (b.26/8/1681, d.8/12/1739).
>
> *General der Kavallerie* (1733) Claudius Petrus von St. Paul, Knight of the St. Heinrich Order.
>
> *General der Infanterie* (1737) Alexander Joseph Graf von Sulkowsky, Cabinet Minister, Knight of the St. Andrew, of the White Eagle and of the St. Heinrich Orders (b.13/3/1695, d.21/5/1762).
>
> *General der Kavallerie* (1737) Friedrich von Zuhlen, Knight of the St. Heinrich Order.
>
> *General der Kavallerie* (1738) Friedrich August Graf von Rutowsky, Knight of the White Eagle and of the St. Heinrich Orders.

General-Lieutenant
> Claudius de Brosses Plenipotentiary in Holland (cavalry).
>
> Karl Friedrich Gottlob Graf von Castell (infantry) Commandant in Dresden
>
> Johann von Bodt, *Chef der Ingenieurs, Ober-Bau Director,* and Commandant of New Dresden
>
> Moritz von Kavanagh (cavalry).
>
> Georg Ignatius Fürst Lubomirsky (cavalry).

Georg Friedrich von Gfug (cavalry) (1733)

Johann Adam von Diemar (infantry) (1733)

Georg Wilhelm von Bircholz (cavalry) (1734)

Wichmann von Klingenberg (cavalry) (1738)

Joh. Baptista von Renard, General-Quartier-Meister (infantry) (1739)

Jacob Alexander, Fürst Lubomirsky (1739)

Generalmajor

Caspar Otto von Glasenapp (cavalry).

Karl Isaac de la Haye (cavalry).

Matthias von Berner (cavalry).

Rudolph Heinrich von Neitschuz (cavalry).

Wolff Adolph von Gersdorff (cavalry).

Hermann, Freiherr von Riedesel, Commandant of Königstein (infantry).

Wolfgang Georg von Marchen, Commandant of the Fortress of Pleissenburg of Lipsia.

George Hubert von Diesbach, Trabanten-Hauptmann (infantry) (1733).

Georg Karl Graf von Zaugwitz (cavalry) (1733).

Karl Heinrich von Grosse (cavalry) (1734).

Christian Ernst von Polenz (cavalry) (1734).

Julius August von Goldacker (cavalry) (1734).

Friedrich Ludewig von Grumbkow (cavalry) (1734) (b. 14/3 /1681, d. 14/3/1745).

Karl Ludwig Prinz von Holstein (cavalry) (1734).

Graf von Flemming, (infantry) (1734).

Karl Andreas von Jasmund (infantry) (1734).

Adam Friedrich Brand von Lindau (cavalry) (1734).

Johann Paul Sybilsky (cavalry) (1735).

Joh. Michael von Schindler (infantry) (1735).

Karl Friedrich von Schonbeck (cavalry) (1735).

Franz, Chevalier von la Sarre (1735).

Christoph von Unruh, *Kriegs Rath* Vice President (1738).

Georg, Chevalier von Sachsen (cavalry) (1738).

Aemilius Friedrich Freiherr von Rochow (infantry) (1739).

Karl Sigmund von Arnim (cavalry) (1739).

Colonels (*Obristen*)

Johann Cristoph von Penzig (cavalry).

Wocislav von Podocki (cavalry).

Johann Heinrich Boblick (cavalry).

Joh. Jacob Glatte (engineers).

Christof Karl von Isenbrand (engineers).

Benno Sigmund von Gersdorff.

Johann Christoph Naumann (engineers), *Ober-Ausseher*, Supervisor of all the Fortifications.

Ludolph Christian, Freiherr von Bothmar (infantry).

Karl Alexander Graf Bose.

Julius Friedrich von Weissbach (infantry).

Karl Wilhelm von Block (cavalry).

Peter l'Hermet von Caila (infantry).

Erdmann, Graf von Promnitz, Cabinet Minister, Knight of the White Eagle (infantry).

Christoph Ernst von Nassau (cavalry).

Georg Asmus von Schonbeck (infantry).

Joachim Heinrich von Durrfeld (cavalry).

Christian Friedrich von Brüchting (infantry).

Christian Wilhelm, Prinz von Sachsen-Gotha, Knight of the White Eagle (cavalry).

Heinrich Gottlob von Oppeln (cavalry).

Dietrich August von Adeleps (infantry).

Joh. Ludewig von Ponickau (cavalry).

Joh. Gottlob Meyer (cavalry).

Joh. Adolph von Liebenau (infantry).

Joh. August, Freiherr von Harthausen (infantry).

Caspar Heinrich von Deutsch (infantry).

Georg Sigmund von Schlichting (cavalry).

Sigmund Gottlob von Mezrad (infantry).

Emanuel von Pomy (cavalry).

Moritz Heinrich von Arnstadt (cavalry).

Friedrich Karl von Bestenbostel (cavalry).

Balthasar Friedrich, Graf von Promnitz (cavalry).

Johann Zacharias von Schlieben (infantry).

Karl Georg Friedrich, Graf von Flemming

Hermann Landsberg (engineers) (1733)

Franz August Robillard von Champagne (1733).

Johann Albrecht von Raguczi (cavalry) (1733).

Wilhelm Ludewig Rouxel von Longrais (engineers) (1733).

Joh. Georg Maxim. Fürstenhof (engineers) (1733).

Stanislaus Alexander, Graf von Sulkowsky (infantry) (1734).

Johann Moritz, Graf von Brühl (cavalry) (1734).

Joh. Cristoph von Minckwitz (infantry) (1734).

Christian Prinz von Schwarzburg-Sondershausen (cavalry) (1734).

Friedrich August Graf von Cosel (infantry) (1734).

Friedrich Gottlob von Milckau (cavalry) (1734).

Joh. Cristoph von Natzmer (infantry) (1734).

Peter von Suhm (infantry) (1734).

Barnabas von O'Dempsie (infantry) (1734).

Joachim Daniel Jauch (engineers) (1735).

Johann von Wilster (artillery) (1735).

Cristoph Levin von Trotta, gennant Trenden, General-Adjutant (1735).

Stanislaus von Storzewsky, General-Adjutant (1735).

Der Herr von Buttler (1735).

Otto Reinhold von Mannteuffel (infantry) (1735).

August Benjamin von Buchner (cavalry) (1735).

Georg Karl von Weissbach (infantry) (1735).

Friedrich Wilhelm von Franckenberg (infantry) (1735).

Johann von Maffei (cavalry) (1735).

Christian von Plötz, General-Adjutant (1736).

Josef von Morlet (cavalry) (1736).

Karl Ernest von Gersdorff (cavalry) (1736).

Joh. Friedrich, Graf Vitzthum von Eckstädt (cavalry) (1736).

Ewald Reimar von Wobeser (infantry) (1736).

Christian Eusebius von Kalckreut (1737)

Karl Joachim von Römer (infantry) (1737).

Joachim Matthias von Carnitz (cavalry) (1738).

Otto Friedrich von Ponickau (cavalry) (1738).

Caspar Franz von Fontenay (cavalry) (1738).

Johann Franz, Graf von Bellegarde (infantry) (1739).

Bernhard von Munchow (1739).

Ludewig von Belleville (infantry) (1739).

Johann Adolph von Alenbeck (1739).

Karl Moritz von Carlowitz (1739).

Sigmund, Graf von Nostitz (cavalry) (1739).

Heinrich von Neubauer (1739).

The Inspectors

Otto Friedrich von Ponickau (cavalry).

Wolff Abraham von Gersdorff (infantry).

Drill Masters (*Exercitienmeister*)

Karl Heinrich von Rechenberg (cavalry) (1733).

Dobislaus Nicolaus von Pirch (infantry) (1733) (b. 29/9/1693, d. 21/4/1768).

Gouverneurs and *Commandanten* of the Fortresses

Gouverneur of Dresden: Heinrich Friedrich Graf von Friesen, Cabinet Minister and *General der Infanterie* (1734).

Gouverneur of Lipsia: Joachim Friedrich Graf von Flemming, *General der Kavallerie.*

Gouverneur of Wittenberg: Adam Heinrich von Bose, *General der Infanterie.*

The Commandant of Dresden: Karl Friedrich Gottlob, Graf von Castell, *General-Lieutenant* (1733).

The Commandant of Neustadt Dresden: Johann von Bodt, *General-Lieutenant* and Chef of the Engineers (1734).

The Commandant of Königstein: Hermann, Freiherr von Riedesel zu Eisenbach, *Generalmajor* (b.1682, d.1751).

The Commandant of Pleissenburg of Lipsia: Wolfgang Georg von Marchen, *Generalmajor.*

The Commandant of Sonnenstein of Pirna: Friedrich Ludewig von Grumbkow, *Generalmajor* (1734).

Appendix III

The Saxon Army 1755

Adeliges Kadettenkorps
Garde du Corps
Karabiniersgarde

Cuirassiers Regiments
1. Leib-Regiment
2. Kurprinz
3. Arnim, also written Arnimb
4. Anhalt-Dessau
5. Ploetze
6. Vitzthum

Chevauxlegers Regiments or Light Dragoon Regiments
1. Prinz Karl
2. Prinz Albrecht
3. Graf Rutowsky
4. Graf Brühl

Artillerie

Infanterie
• Leib-Grenadiergarde
• Garde zu Fuss
• Königin
• Chur-Prinzessin Grenadierbattalion
• Prinz Xaver
• Prinz Clemens
• Prinz Friedrich August
• Prinz Karl Maximilian
• Prinz Gotha
• Minckwitz
• Rochow
• Graf Brühl
• Fürst Lubomirsky

Appendix IV

Saxon Army Staff 1760

Feldmarschall, Commander-in-Chief:

- Friedrich August, Graf von Rutowsky, Governor of Dresden, *Obrist-Haus-Zeugmeister* and *Obrist-Land-Zeugmeister*.

Generals
- Alexander Joseph, Prinz Sulkowsky (infantry).
- Georg, Chevalier von Sachsen (cavalry).
- Heinrich, Graf von Brühl (infantry).
- Jacob Alexander, Fürst Lubomirsky (infantry).
- Karl Sigmund von Arnim (cavalry).
- Christoph, Graf von Unruh (infantry), President of the War Council and Commander of Neustadt near Dresden.
- Johann August, Baron von Harthausen (infantry), Governor of Leipzig
- Johann Paul Sybilsky, Baron von Wolfsberg (cavalry).
- Friedrich August, Graf von Cosel (infantry).
- Johann von Wilster (infantry).
- Eugen von Anhalt-Dessau (cavalry), Governor of Wittenberg.

General-Lieutenant
- Karl Ludwig, Prinz von Holstein (cavalry).
- Karl Georg Friedrich Graf von Flemming (infantry).
- Michael Lorenz von Pirch (infantry), Commander of Königstein.
- Thaddäus de Meagher (infantry), Captain of the Swiss Lifeguards.
- Johann Franz, Graf von Bellegarde (infantry).
- Christian von Plötz (cavalry).
- Johann Friedrich, Graf Vitzthum von Eckstädt (cavalry).
- Karl Gottlob von Minckwitz (cavalry).
- Friedrich Wilhelm von Rex (cavalry).
- Johann Adolph, Prinz von Sachsen-Gotha (infantry).
- Heinrich Christoph, Graf von Baudissin (infantry).
- Peter von Suhm (infantry).
- Georg Dietrich von Münnich (infantry).
- Debislav Nicolaus von Pirch (infantry).

- Stanislaus von Skorzewsky (cavalry).
- Wolf Caspar von Zeschwitz (cavalry).
- Friedrich Christoph zu Solms (infantry).

Generalmajor

- Francois, Chevalier de la Serre (infantry).
- Johann Ludwig von Ponickau (cavalry).
- Georg Karl von Weissbach (cavalry).
- F. Bode, Graf von Stolberg-Rossla (infantry).
- Caspar Franz von Fontenay (cavalry)
- Johann von Chur Sachsen (arm of service unknown)
- Johann Jacob von O'Byrn (cavalry).
- Johann August von Gersdorff (infantry).
- Karl Heinrich von Rechenberg, Inspector of Cavalry and Infantry.
- Ä. Bledowski (cavalry).
- Louis, Baron de Belleville (infantry), Commander of the Fortress of Pleissenburg near Leipzig.
- Christian Friedrich Erndl (engineers).
- Christoph Heinrich Vitzthum von Eckstädt (cavalry).
- Christoph Erdmann von Reitzenstein (cavalry).
- Wolf Heinrich von Bolberitz (infantry).
- Joh. Wilhelm, Graf von Ronnow (cavalry).
- Christian Ludwig Wilhelm von Nischwitz (engineers and inspector)
- Otto Friedrich von Ponickau (cavalry).
- Franz Noa von Crousatz (infantry).
- Antoine von Monette (arm of service unknown).
- Johann Adolph von Liebenau (infantry), Commander of Stolpen.
- August Sigismund von Zeuzsch (cavalry).
- Franz Theodor, Baron von Stain (cavalry).
- Johann Friedrich von Dallwitz (cavalry).
- Johann Friedrich von Dieden (infantry).
- Georg Wilhelm von Hardenberg (cavalry).
- Hanns Caspar von Schlieben (infantry).
- Johann von Monro (cavalry).
- Ludwig, Baron von Rochow (infantry), Commander of Sonnenstein.
- Georg Wilhelm Kändler (infantry).
- Moritz August, Baron von Spörken (arm of service unknown)
- Augüst Constanz, Graf von Nostitz (infantry).
- Maximilian von der Pahlen (infantry).
- Ludwig von Galbert (cavalry).
- Johann Hermann, Graf von der Horst (infantry).
- Hanns Daniel Wilhelm von Geyer (engineers)
- Karl Wilhelm von Bomsdorf (infantry).
- Mauritius d'Elbee (arm of service unknown).
- Christian Friedrich von Brüchting (infantry).
- Wolf Heinrich von Gößnitz (cavalry).
- Andreas, Graf von Renard (uhlans).
- Wichmann, Baron von Klingenberg (infantry).

Colour Plate Commentaries

Plate A: Saxon General Staff mid-18th Century

A1: Friedrich August, Graf von Rutowsky wearing the pale yellow and crimson uniform of *Oberst* of the Saxon Regiment Leibgrenadiergarde, in 1730.

Friedrich August (born 19 June 1702, died 16 March 1764 at Pillnitz, Saxony) was an illegitimate son of Augustus II the Strong, King of Poland and Elector of Saxony. He inherited his father's name and his characteristic thick eyebrows. His mother was the Turk Fatima (or Fatime), who had been captured in 1686 by Hans Adam von Schöning during the Battle of Buda. After she became the King's mistress, Fatima was christened Maria Anna and moved to the Dresden court. After the birth, Fatima was married, at the instigation of Augustus, to his chamber man Johann Georg von Spiegel. Friedrich August moved to the estates of the Spiegel Family, but his father cared about his education. Fatima, despite her marriage, remained a mistress of Augustus. In 1706, she gave birth to the King's second child, a daughter, called Maria Anna Katharina. However, soon Friedrich August and his sister became orphans: Johann Georg von Spiegel died in 1715 and their mother Fatima five years later. Augustus the Strong took the guardianship of the children.

In 1724, Augustus the Strong recognized and legitimized the two children he had had with Fatima. Shortly after, he raised both, in his capacity as King of Poland, to the Polish title of Graf von Rutowsky and Graffin Rutowska. The coat of arms awarded to them shows a Saxon rhombus wreath as well as a Polish White Eagle. On 8 October of the same year, Friedrich August, now Graf von Rutowsky, received from his father the highest Polish decoration: the Order of the White Eagle. He had the rank of *Oberst* in the Saxon Army. After a journey to Munich and Venice, Rutowsky arrived in February 1725 at the court of the King of Sardinia and Duke of Savoy, Victor Amadeus II, in Turin, where he took command of the Piedmont regiment and was garrisoned in Alessandria. He really enjoyed his time there, and maybe that was the reason why he wrote his father asking to give to him the permission to enter in French service in order to remain in Turin. His father had different plans for his son, and demanded his immediate return. On 26 May 1727, Rutowsky was appointed *Generalmajor* in the Saxon Army but, shortly after we find him in the service of the Prussian King (in Regiment von Thiele). He learnt his lesson perfectly. In 1729, the General Graf von Rutowsky was again in Saxon service and in 1730 received the command of the Leibgrenadiergarde. The same year, as a reward for his action in the reform of the Saxon Army, Rutowsky was put in charge of the Saxon Leibgrenadiergarde defiling at the summer camp in Zeithain. It was the European military 'event' of the year. The best compliment to General Rutowsky was the acid comment of the Prussian 'Sergeant King' Friedrich Wilhelm I: '*Die Canaille hat uns alles abgestohlen*' or 'The villain has stolen everything from us'.

In 1733, Augustus the Strong died suddenly. The new Elector Friedrich August II was Rutowsky's half-brother. During the War of the Polish Succession, Rutowsky participated in the campaigns in Poland and on the Rhine. On 1 January 1736, Rutowsky was appointed *General-Lieutenant* and commander of Garde du Corps (see Plate E). In 1737, Rutowsky was the leader of the Saxon Contingent in the war against the Turks in Hungary. On 21 April 1738, Rutowsky was appointed *General der Kavallerie*. On 4 January 1739, he married with Princess Ludovika Amalie Lubomirska. Their only child, August Joseph, Graf von Rutowsky (born 2 August 1741) died of smallpox in Brunswick on 17 January 1755.

In 1741, Rutowsky commanded the Saxon army that besieged Prague, and campaigned in Bohemia and Moravia until the Siege of Brunn. On 10 January 1742, he was appointed Proprietor of a newly raised chevauxlegers or light dragoon regiment. During the Second Silesian War, Sachsen-Weissenfels was Saxon commander in chief but was replaced by Rutowsky, for health reasons, few days before the battle of Kesselsdorf. The Elector removed his half-brother Rutowsky from command and reinstated Sachsen-Weissenfels.

On 6 January 1746, after Sachsen-Weissenfels' death, Rutowsky was appointed *General en Chef*. On 11 January 1749, Rutowsky was appointed *Feldmarschall*. During the following years of peace, Rutowsky was not able, despite multiple efforts, to avert the cutbacks in the Saxon Army by Prime Minister Brühl, which seriously reduced its effectiveness. In 1756, at the sudden outbreak of the Seven Years War, Rutowsky had in his hands a blunted weapon. He simply had no chance against the advancing Prussian Army. During the Prussian invasion of Saxony, Rutowsky concentrated the Saxon Army of only 18,100 men in the strong defensive position near Pirna. He withstood a siege of 6 weeks, but lacking food and ammunition, he had to capitulate on 16 October 1756. During the years of war, Rutowsky stayed in Saxony. On 8 March 1763, just after the Treaty of Hubertusburg, Rutowsky renounced all his military functions. He died one year later, aged 62. On 27 July 1764, his half-brother and historical second-in-command, Johann Georg, Chevalier de Saxe (1704–1774) succeeded him at the head of the Saxon Army (see Plate B2).

A2: Friedrich August II, Elector of Saxony, around 1740.

Elector of Saxony (1733–1763); King of Poland, as Augustus III (1734–1763); and Grand Duke of Lithuania, as Augustus III (1734–1763) was born on 17 October 1696 in Dresden. Friedrich August was the only legitimate son of Augustus the Strong, Elector of Saxony and King of the Polish-Lithuanian Commonwealth, who belonged to the Albertine line of the House of Wettin. His mother was Christiane Eberhardine of Brandenburg-Bayreuth. Groomed to succeed his father as king of Poland, Augustus converted to Catholicism in 1712; when publicly announced, this caused discontent among the Protestant Saxon aristocracy. Upon the death of Augustus II in 1733, Augustus inherited the Saxon Electorate and was elected to the Polish throne, with the support of the Russian Empire and the Holy Roman Empire.

As king and elector, Friedrich August was uninterested in the affairs of his Electorate of Saxony and of his Polish–Lithuanian Dominion, focusing instead on hunting, the opera, and the collection of artwork. He resided mainly in Saxony, spending less than three years of his 30-year reign in Poland. Friedrich August delegated most of his powers and responsibilities in the Commonwealth to Heinrich von Brühl, who served in effect as the viceroy of Poland.

At the outbreak of the Seven Years War, the Saxon Army entrenched itself at Pirna. On September 8, as the Prussians were approaching Dresden, Friedrich August left the city with his two sons, Prinz Xaver and Prinz Karl, and his dignitaries. They all joined the troops at Pirna where the Saxons capitulated on October 16. On Wednesday October 20, the Elector set out from Königstein fortress for Warsaw while his queen remained in Dresden. On October 27, Friedrich August arrived in Warsaw where he remained, in relative political impotence, till the end of the war. Friedrich August II died on 5 October 1763 soon after his return to Dresden. His eldest surviving son, Friedrich Christian succeeded him as elector.

Plate B: Saxon General Staff mid-18th century

B1: Graf Heinrich von Brühl in uniform of a *General-Lieutenant* after the portrait by the Roman painter Marcello Bacciarelli.

Heinrich, Graf von Brühl (13 August 1700 – 28 October 1763), one of the most controversial personalities of his age, was born in Gangloffsömmern the son of Johann Moritz von Brühl, a noble who held the office of *Oberhofmarschall* at the court of Saxe-Weissenfels, and his first wife Erdmuth Sophie von der Heide. His father was ruined and compelled to part with his family estate, which passed into the hands of the prince. Under Duke Christian of Saxe-Weissenfels, von Brühl was first placed as a page with the dowager duchess, and was then received at her recommendation into the court of the Electorate of Saxony at Dresden as a *Silberpage* on 16 April 1719. He rapidly acquired the favour of the Augustus the Strong. Brühl was particularly able in procuring money for his master. He became Chief Receiver of Taxes and Minister of the

Interior of Saxony in 1731. He was at Warsaw when his master died in 1733, and rapidly managed to obtain the confidence of the new Elector by acquiring the papers and jewels of the dead King and bringing them promptly to his successor. Von Brühl raised money to secure the election of Friedrich August II as Polish king. During most of the thirty years of the reign of Augustus III, he remained the major confidant of the king and the *de facto* head of the Saxon court. Reichsgraf since 27 November 1737, after 1738 he was in effect sole minister. Brühl had cunning and skill sufficient to govern his master and succeeded in keeping everybody at a distance from the king. No servant entered the king's service without the consent of Brühl, and even when the king went to the chapel any approach to him was prevented.

The firm grip on his master was possible thanks to the perpetual and insatiable passion of the King for art collection. It was not until the beginning of the 18th century that Augustus the Strong and his son started to collect paintings systematically. Over a period of less than 60 years, these two art-loving Electors expanded the collections significantly. Curious anecdotes about the Elector's insane passion circulated at the Dresden court, true or not. Every year, for the King-Elector's birthdays the Queen used to buy a painting for her beloved husband. Once, she acquired instead an exquisitely chiselled tobacco box. The Elector was receiving the expensive present when he candidly said: 'Where is my painting?' It seems that a typical interaction of the Elector with Brühl has the Elector loitering about, smoking, and asking, without looking at his favourite, 'Brühl, have I any money?' 'Yes, sire,' was the continual answer. To satisfy the king's demands, Brühl moved huge sum of money, exhausting both Saxony and the Polish Commonwealth. The countries plunged into debts and to reduce the expenses von Brühl greatly reduced the army. Consequently, he was wholly responsible for a fiscal policy that weakened the position of Saxony within the Holy Roman Empire between 1733 and 1763.

In 1736, the architect Johann Christoph Knöffel had begun to build a city palace and terrace for Brühl on the bank of the Elbe in the heart of Dresden. This was originally called Brühl's Garden and is today known as Brühl's Terrace. In 1746, the title of a Prime Minister was created for Brühl, the first time in Saxony, making him the second man of the State, but as a classic court favourite his power extended beyond that office. Besides securing huge grants of land for himself, he acquired numerous titles, and he drew the combined salaries of these offices. He also worked closely with Bishop Kajetan Sołtyk of Kraków.

Heinrich von Brühl competed with his master also as a collector. It is widely believed that Brühl had Europe's largest collection of watches and military vests; attributed to him was also a vast collection of ceremonial wigs, hats, shoes and the largest collection of Meissen porcelain in the world. Brühl was a general and proprietor of both an infantry and a chevauxlegers regiment in the Saxon Army. He kept 200 domestics; his guards were better paid than those of the king himself, and his table more sumptuous. Friedrich II of Prussia, who developed during the years a personal hate for him, said: 'Brühl had more garments, watches, laces, boots, shoes and slippers, than any man of the age. Caesar would have counted him among those curled and perfumed heads which he did not fear'. Francesco Algarotti called him a Maecenas. He owned a large gallery of pictures, which was bought by Empress Catherine II of Russia in 1768, and his library of 70,000 volumes was one of the biggest private libraries in the Holy Roman Empire. His profusion, if disastrous for the army was beneficial to the arts and sciences. The famous Meissen porcelain Swan Service was made for him, with over 2,200 pieces, now dispersed to collections around the world.

The passion of the Elector was insatiable and in 1745, after the disaster of Kesselsdorf, the 100 best pieces of the collection belonging to the Duke of Modena (Francesco III) were purchased for the fabulous sum of 100,000 golden florins. The collection arrived in Dresden the following year. As the fast-growing painting collection soon required more space for storage and presentation, it was moved from Dresden Castle to the adjacent *Stallgebäude* (the Electors' Stables Building) in 1747. In the meantime, the collection had achieved European fame. Paintings from all over Europe, especially from Italy, Paris, Amsterdam, and Prague, were acquired and sent to Dresden. The purchasing activities were crowned by the acquisition of Raphael's *Sistine Madonna* in 1754. In 1754, Friedrich August purchased the painting for 110,000–120,000 francs, whereupon it was relocated to Dresden and achieved new prominence. This was to remain the highest price paid for any painting for many decades. If the stories are correct, the painting achieved its prominence immediately, as it is said that Augustus moved his throne to better display it.

Brühl, as a diplomat, played a vital role in the Diplomatic Revolution of 1756 and the convergence of the Habsburg Empire and France, but the Seven Years War was a disaster for Saxony, which remained a war theatre for the rest of the conflict. Outside the art market, Heinrich Brühl had no friends. At the French court in Paris, he was considered not only without political or military capacity, but so garrulous that he could not keep a secret. His indiscretion was repeatedly responsible for the King of Prussia's discoveries of the plans laid against him. Anyway, nothing could shake the confidence of his master, which survived the ignominious flight into Bohemia, at the time of the Battle of Kesselsdorf, and all the miseries of the Seven Years War.

The favourite abused the confidence of his master shamelessly. Not content with the 67,000 thalers a month, which he drew as salary for his innumerable offices, he was found when an inquiry was held in the next reign to have abstracted more than five million thalers of public money for his private use. He left the work of the government offices to his lackeys, whom he did not even supervise. Brühl died at Dresden on 28 October 1763, having survived his master only for a few weeks. The new elector, Friedrich Christian caused an inquiry to be held into his administration. His fortune including large palaces at Pförten (present day Brody), Oberlichtenau and Wachau-Seifersdorf was found to amount to a million and a half thalers , and was sequestered but afterwards restored to his family. The inquiry showed that Brühl owed his immense fortune to the prodigality of the king rather than to unlawful means of accumulation.

B2: Johann Georg von Sachsen (aka Chevalier de Saxe) as *General-Lieutenant der Kavallerie*, 1744.

Johann Georg was born on 21 August 1704, at Dresden, Saxony. He was an illegitimate son of Augustus the Strong and Ursula Katharina of Altenbockum, by marriage Princess Lubomirska. At that time, the Lubomirsky family was ranked among the most influential families of Poland. He received from his father the name Johann Georg and the characteristic features of thick eyebrows. A few days after his birth, his mother was created Princess of Teschen. Johann Georg grew up in his mother's houses in Dresden and in Breslau (present day Wroclaw). In 1714, the 34-year-old Princess Lubomirska was back again in Dresden where she lived receiving a pension. On September 1718, Johann Georg moved to Rome. He received a complete education by the Jesuits, like a large part of the Noble Cadets of the age. At first, he received the title of Prince of Teschen and, by an express desire of his mother, Johann Georg started a spiritual/political career. He entered into the Order of Malta or Knights of Malta (a Roman Catholic lay religious order, traditionally of military, chivalrous and noble nature). In 1722, Johann Georg received the Great Cross of the Order of Malta. His title was soon changed to the Chevalier de Saxe.

In December 1724, Johann left Rome. He was accompanied by the Saxon *Oberst-Lieutenant* Barnabas O'Dempsie to Lunéville, where he was received to the residence of the Duke von Löthringen. In May 1726, by order of the Grand Master of the Order, Johann Georg was sent to Malta. In October 1727, however, Johann Georg left the Order and was recalled to Dresden. His father had different plans for him. On January 8 1728, Johann Georg was awarded the Polish Order of the White Eagle and on 12 December 1729, Johann Georg was appointed the rank of *Oberst* in the Saxon Army. On 1 January 1730, Johann Georg became commander and proprietor of the former Dragoon Regiment von Klingenberg, now Dragoon Regiment Chevalier de Saxe. The unit was on garrison service in Lubben. The same year, Johann Georg was present at the summer camp in Zeithain.

The garrison service ended when his father suddenly died. The Saxon Army and the Chevalier de Saxe regiment moved to Poland to 'support' the election of his half-brother Friedrich August II as King of Poland. During the ensuing Polish Succession War, the Saxon Army remained in Poland for three years. On 7 September 1738, Johann Georg was appointed *Generalmajor der Kavallerie* and on 11 August 1740 was promoted to the rank of *General-Lieutenant der Kavallerie*. On September 1 of the same year, he was recalled in Dresden to assume the command of the elite regiment of Garde du Corps. After the capitulation at Pirna, Johann Georg, free on parole, spent the years of war in Dresden like his half-brother and superior officer Graf von Rutowsky.

On 27 July 1763, after Rutowsky's death, Johann Georg von Sachsen was appointed as *Feldmarschall* and Governor of Dresden. Johann Georg was 59 years old. On 18 August of the same year, he was appointed as *Direktor des Geheimen Kriegs-Kollegiums* and *Generaldirektor der Kriegkasse*. After the long struggle of three successive wars, a reform of the Saxon Army became a priority. The task was initiated under the short reign of the new Elector of Saxony Friedrich Christian by his brother Xaver de Saxe and continued during the Regency. On 27 November 1764 Johann Georg acquired the so-called *Zinzendorfschen Garden*, located out of the gates of the city of Dresden, for the sum of 14,000 thalers. In the middle of the garden, a magnificent palace in rococo style was built up, by the later garden-master builder Friedrich August Krubsacius. This palace was (after the Moszinskapalais and the Brühlschen Palais in Dresden-Friedrichstadt) the third 'Maison de Plaisance' of the aristocracy out the city walls of Dresden. In 1774, after a long disease, the Chevalier de Saxe died aged sixty-nine. He was buried in the Roman Catholic Cemetery (*Innerer Katholischen Friedhof*) in Dresden. In his will, the Chevalier declared his half-sister, Friedricha Alexandrine, Graffin von Cosel (by marriage Graffin Moszinska) his sole heir.

Plate C: Schweizerleibgarde (Swiss Lifeguards)

Augustus the Strong was an admirer of King Louis XIV and consequently the Saxon *Trabanten* were modelled after the French *Cent-Suisses*, the personal Swiss Bodyguards of the French King. This 100 men strong Corps served his successor loyally also in the hard circumstances of the Seven Years War.

C1: A Swiss Lifeguard wearing the service German uniform.

C2: A Swiss Lifeguard wearing the gala Swiss uniform.

C3: A Swiss Lifeguard after a plate from a manuscript of the Deutsches Historisches Museum in Berlin, showing a Swiss Guard wearing the *mantel* (greatcoat) over the German uniform in 1756.

Plate D: Adeliges Kadettenkorps (Corps des *Cadets-gentilhommes*)

D1: 1756. Cadet in service dress.

D2: 1756. Cadet in gala dress.

Plate E: Garde du Corps

E1: Officer of the Garde du Corps between 1734 and 1738.

E2: *Trabant* (horseman) of the Garde du Corps between 1735 and 1738.

Plate F: Saxon Garde du Corps

F1: Staff officer of the Regiment Garde du Corps in Gala dress with '*supraveste*'.

Plate G: Cuirassiers regiments, 1756

G1: Cuirassiers Regiment Rechenberg/von Anhalt-Dessau, 1748–1756, *General-Lieutenant* Friedrich Heinrich Eugen von Anhalt-Dessau (1705–1781), proprietor of the cavalry unit, in combat dress, 1756.

Friedrich Heinrich Eugen von Anhalt-Dessau was a German prince of the House of Ascania from the Anhalt-Dessau branch. He was born on 27 December 1705 in Dessau as the fourth son of Leopold I, Fürst von Anhalt-Dessau, the famous Prussian general known as 'the Old Dessauer' and of his morganatic wife Anna Louise Föse. He was the cousin of Friedrich II of Prussia. In 1717, at the age of only twelve, Eugen joined the Prussian Army with the rank of *Rittmeister*, rising to the rank of *Generalmajor* by 1740. Eugen took part in the First Silesian War but, after the unsuccessful combat at Kranowitz on 20 May 1742, was criticized by King Friedrich II and, on 8 January 1744, abandoned his charge in the Prussian Army, left the Prussian service, and joined the Austrian Army under the command of Prinz Karl von Löthringen as a volunteer on the Rhine.

In June 1746, Eugen joined the Army of the Electorate of Saxony, where he became in February 1749 governor of Wittenberg. In 1749, Eugen was appointed *chef* of the former Cuirassier Regiment Schwarzburg-Sondershausen, a charge that he would retain until his death. In 1754, Eugen was promoted to *General der Kavallerie*. In 1756, during the Prussian invasion of Saxony, Eugen commanded a brigade of cuirassiers. On October 16, he surrendered with the rest of the Saxon army at Pirna. Freed under parole, he refused to serve in the Prussian Army. In January 1775, Eugen was promoted to Saxon *Feldmarschall*. In the War of the Bavarian Succession, he led the Saxons attached to the Prussian Corps of General Dubislaw von Platen. Eugen never married or had children, and never took part in the government of Anhalt-Dessau. He died on 2 March 1781 in Dessau.

G2: Cuirassier Regiment von Vitzthum, horseman 1748–1756.

G3: Leib-Cuirassier Regiment, horseman 1748–1756.

Plate H: Chevauxlegers Regiment, 1756

H1: Mounted dragoon of Prinz Albrecht Chevauxlegers in combat dress, 1756.

Bibliography

Anon., *Accurate Vorstellung der sämtlichen ChurFürstl: Sächß. Regimenter und Corps: Worinnen zur eigentl: Kenntniß der Uniform von jedem Regimente Ein Officier und Ein Gemeiner in völliger Montirung und ganzer Statur nach dem Leben abgebildet sind* (Nürnberg: Raspe, 1769)

Anon., *Ihre Königl. Majestät in Pohlen und Chur – Fürstl. Duchl. zu Sachsen etc. allergnädigst approbiertes Dienst-Reglement im Lande und im Felde vor Dero Infanterie-Regimenter* (Dresden: Stösselin, 1753)

Anon. [Bachenschwanz, L.], *Geschichte und gegenwärtiger Zustand der Kursächsischen Armee* 2nd edition, part IX (Dresden: Bachenschwanz, 1793)

Anon. *Koenigl.Pohln. und Chur-Fuersten Sachsen zu oservirende neue Hof-Rang Ordnung* (Dresden, n.p., 1755)

Anon., *Stamm- und Rangliste der Koenigl. Sächsischen Armee auf das Jahr 1803* (Dresden: n.p., 1803)

Anon., 'Uniformes Prussien et Saxonne' (Berlin: Manuskript Deutsches Historisches Museum, 1756/57)

d'Archenholtz, J.W., *Histoire de la guerre de Sept ans an Allemagne de 1756 à 1763* (Berne: Haller, 1789)

Barth, Joh. A., *Pragmatische Geschichte der Saechsischen Truppen, ein Taschenbuch für Soldaten* (Leipzig: Barth, 1792)

von Beust, *Feldzuege der chursaechsischen Truppen* (N.p.: n.p., n.d.)

Cagnat, Lieut., *Journal des Marches et de Combats du Regiment d'Anjou-infanterie* (Paris: Ed. Lavauzelle, n.d.)

D.M.V.L.N., *Histoire de la derniere guerre de Boheme* (Frankfort, Lenclume 1747)

Duffy, C., The army of Frederick the Great, (Chicago IL: Emperor's Press, 1996 2nd ed.)

Dussauge, A., *Etudes sur la Guerre de Sept ans. Le Ministere Belle-isle. Krefeldt et Lutterberg.* (Paris: Ed. Fournier, 1914)

Großer Generalstab, Kriegsgeschichtliche Abteilung II, *Die Kriege Friedrichs des Großen. Dritter Teil: Der Siebenjährige Krieg 1756–1763. Vol. 1 Pirna und Lobositz* (Berlin: Mittler, 1901)

Hasse F. & Johannes Eichorn (after R. Trache), *Sächsische Uniformen* (Großenhain: n.p., 1936–1942)

Hauthal, Ferdinand, *Geschichte der sächsische Armee in Wort und Bild* (Leipzig: J.G. Bach, 1859)

Henne, J.C., *Journal von 21 September 1757 bis zum 26 Juli 1758 betreffend der Marsch einiger hundert Reverdenten von Prag ueber Brunn nach Ungarn* (Freiberg: n.p., 1772)

Hohrath, Daniel, *The Uniforms of the Prussian Army under Frederick the Great from 1740 to 1786* (Vienna: Verlag Militaria, 2011)

Knötel, Herbert d.J. & Brauer Hans M., *Heer und Tradition, Heeres-Uniformbogen* (so-called "Brauer-Bogen") (Berlin: Verlag Brauer, 1926 -1962)

Knötel, Richard, *Uniformenkunde, Lose Blätter zur Geschichte der Entwicklung der militärischen Tracht* (Rathenow: Babenzien, 1890–1921)

von Kretschmar, A., *Geschichte der Kurfuerstlich und Koeniglich Saechsischen Feld-Artillerie von 1620-1820* (Berlin: Mittler, 1879)

de Lostelneau, Colbert, *Le maréschal de Bataille* (Paris: Estienne Mignon, 1647)

Lützow, L. von, *Die Schlacht von Hohenfriedberg oder Striegau am 4 Juni 1745* (Potsdam: Riegel, 1845)

von Marees, G., 'Das Saechsische-Polnische Cavalleriecorps in Oesterreichischen Solde von 1756 bis 1763', *Jahrbücher fur die Deutsche Armee und Marine* XXVIII Band 1878

de Martange, *Correspondance inedite du General Major de Martange* (Paris: A. Picard et fils,1898)

Müller, Reinhold, Manfred Lachmann & Wolfgang Friedrich, *Spielmann-Trompeter-Hoboist.* (Berlin: Militärverlag der DDR, 1988)

Müller, Reinhold & Wolfgang Friedrich, *Die Armee Augusts des Starken: Das Sächsische Heer von 1730–1733* (Berlin: Militärverlag der DDR, 1984)

Rutowski, Friedrich-Heinrich (hrsg.), *Exercier-Reglement Vor die Königl. Pohln. und Churfürstl. Sächßl. Infanterie* (Dresden: n.p., 1751)

de Saxe, Maurice, *Mes Reveries* (Leipzig: Arkstée & Merkus,1757)

Sautai, M., *Les debuts de la Guerre de Succession d'Austriche* (Paris, Chapelot 1910)

Schimpff, Georg von, *Die ersten Chur-sachsichen Leibwachen zu Ross und zu Fuss* (Dresden: Baensch, 1894)

Schirmer, Friedrich, *Die Heere der kriegführenden Staaten 1756–1763* (Magstadt: Baden-Württemberg KLIO-Landesgruppe e.V., 1989)

Schuster, O. & F.A. Francke, *Geschichte der Sächsischen Armee von deren Errichtung bis auf die neueste Zeit, Erster Theil* (Leipzig: Duncker & Humblot, 1885)

Staudinger K., *Geschichte des Bayerischen Heeres* (Munich: Lindauer, 1909)

Summerfield, S., *Saxon Artillery 1733–1827* (Nottingham: Partizan Press, 2009)

Summerfield, S., *Saxon Army of the Austrian War of Succession and the Seven Years War* (Godmanchester: Ken Trotman, 2011)

Todiere, M., *L'Autriche sous Marie-Therese* (Rouen: Ed. Megard, 1855)

de Villermont, Cte, *Marie-Therese 1717–1780* (Paris: Desclee,1895)

Wagner, Siegbert: 'Die Uniformen der kursächischen Armee im Jahre 1745' (Hannover: Manuskript, 1979)

Weber, H., *Militaergeschichte des Churfuerstenthums Saechsen und Ihrer Koenigliechen Majestaet in Pohlen 1613–1733* (Dresden: Verlag für sächsische Regionalgeschichte, 2008)

Weber, H., *Militaergeschichte des Churfuerstenthums Saechsen 1733–1763* (Dresden: Verlag für sächsische Regionalgeschichte, 2009)

Wolfgang, Friedrich, 'Kursächische Uniformen zur Zeit der Schlacht bei Kesseldorf', *Zeitschrift für Heereskunde,* vol. LXV (2001) No. 399, Januar/März, pp.8–14; No. 400, April/Juni, pp.41–49; No. 401, Juli/September, pp.92–100

Wolfgang, Friedrich, 'Zur Uniformierung sächsischer Militärmusiker 1733–1756', *Zeitschrift für Heereskunde,* No. 349, Mai/Juni, vol. LIV (1990), pp.81–86

Wolfgang, Friedrich, 'Kursächische Grenadiermützen vor und im Siebenjährigen Krieg', *Zeitschrift für Heereskunde*, No. 373, Juli/September, vol. LVIII (1994), pp.100–103

Wolfgang, Friedrich, *Die Uniformen der Kurfürstlich Sächsichen Armee 1683–1763* (Dresden: Arbeitskreis Sächsische Militärgeschichte, 1998)